Spring forth

By

Mercy Fakoya,
Debbie Akinkunle,
and a few friends

This devotional handbook is dedicated to our children, those we are privileged to mentor (which include the friends who have contributed to this handbook) and those who desire to grow and fall deeply in love with the Living Word of God.

Foreword

It is such an honour to be asked by Mercy and Debbie to write a foreword to this wonderful collection of devotional writings. I have a lot of respect for anyone who writes a devotional.

Devotionals are borne out of the deep spiritual interactions of the writers with the spiritual Manna, the inspired Holy Scriptures. The word of God as recorded for us in the Holy Bible, contains the tools and instructions that we need to successfully navigate the journey of life. The history, stories, chronicles, poems and other writings contained in the Scriptures, have such great diversities of styles and contents that are meant to instruct, inspire and motivate us to live righteous and purposeful lives for all readers who dare to spend time to meditate on them.

Mercy and Debbie, no doubt, have spent a considerable length of time, energy and efforts upon The Holy Scriptures. The result of these is what you will experience as you go through this beautiful, yet impactful and easy to read devotional.

Indeed, it is obvious that they found the time to lay their heads on the Bosom of the Father and worked with the Glorious Holy Spirit through the Scriptures, to let them into HIS Mind. I believe that they actually succeeded, to a very large extent in bringing from the Mind of The Father, some beautiful revelations and insights. They did not just make this happen for themselves alone, but through this awesome devotional, they are unselfishly allowing us to share in the beauty and power of these insights.

I believe that their utmost desire and expectation is that maybe, just maybe, one of us (the readers) would be able to have a peep into the Beautiful Heart of our Glorious Father as we read these writings. The result of this "spiritual peeping" would be a life filled with Godly wisdom and instructions, leading to a glorious and successful Christian Pilgrimage, helping us to arrive HOME eventually and reconnect with our Heavenly Father. For HOME is with the FATHER.

I hereby commend this beautiful and insightful devotional to you; yes, you the one chosen by God to come across it, in an unusual way.

God bless you. In His Love and Mercy always,

Pastor Akinola Soroye

RCCG Victory Centre,
London, England

Introduction

Being a Christian in today's society is hard! That's the honest truth. It's not fashionable at all and if it were to be, it would be fashionable for all the wrong reasons. A vital principle to Christian living is spending time in the word of God; 'relationship over religion' can only be attainable in our lives when we have a healthy habit of delving into the word of God and living it out in our daily lives.

Unfortunately for a lot of people, spending time with God and reading the word is 'hit and miss'. We know we should do it but either don't, or we are just not disciplined enough to stay committed. For some, the reality of the problem faced is not knowing how to spend that 'alone time' with God or what to focus on; so, we get bored, frustrated and tired.

The struggle to *fit* God into our daily schedule is real; after all, life happens - right? Essentially, we know the right thing to do but mostly only engage the word of God in devotion in our own time and when it's convenient to do so, thanks to the many distractions and 'viable' excuses of our times that constantly compete for our attention.

We are two sisters who live some 5000 miles apart, yet in our struggles to devote some meaningful time to God each day, we started to look for a solution and found some solace in devotions. We realized that our struggle to spend quality time with God was eased when we made God the focal point, fitting our schedule around Him rather than the other way around. Everything else began to make sense when we refocused and rescheduled and put God in the centre. Though we both live very busy lifestyles, we became more organised and were able to live more peaceful, even in the midst of chaos.

There are thousands of devotions around, and we have benefited greatly by spending time reading many of them, however, the vision for this devotional handbook which you are now reading came about as the Spirit of God led us to expand on those things we had learnt, and consider practical application too. God also used our life experiences to teach us in our moments of devotion, some of which we share with you through this devotional handbook.

We believe that when God was pouring into us specifically for this devotional handbook, He was thinking about you. Though we have written from our own personal encounters and experiences, we strongly believe that God had you in mind as we penned each page. With every chapter in mind, He considered how it would bring peace your way in the midst of the storm, how it would draw you closer to Him on a daily basis, how it would set you free and break chains that have kept you bound for decades.

This devotional handbook is God's reminder to you that He is still working in you, and through you - your story isn't over, you are about to **SPRING FORTH!** It is our prayer that as you commit to reading it daily, a greater yearning will develop in your heart to delve deeper into the study of the word of God and have or develop your own personal relationship with Him.

This devotional handbook is a start, perhaps the ignition you need to start or restart that daily fellowship with God. There are a total of 50 devotions within this handbook from both of us, and our friends, which you can read in any order. There is also a planner at the back of this book where you can mark each daily devotional as you read.

We pray that as you read through this devotion that:

1. Your heart will be open to receive and connect with God in a fresh way.

2. Your spiritual eyes will be opened to see beyond the words that we have written.

3. Your spiritual ears will be opened to hear what the spirit of God has to say to you concerning your life and His plan and perfect will for your life.

4. There will be a fresh or renewed yearning and passion for the word of God, and you will begin/continue to grow in the knowledge and wisdom of God.

5. Your spiritual growth will be accelerated.

Father, we ask that as this vessel flips through the pages of this devotion, we pray that a transformation and encounter like never before will **SPRING FORTH** within them. We ask that he or she will experience You in a fresh way and a floodgate of unimaginable testimonies will begin to yield as his or her eyes behold every single word on every single page in this devotional handbook.

In Jesus name, Amen

With love,

Debbie Akinkunle & Mercy Fakoya

By the way, we want you to know that as we are privileged to live in the United States of America (USA) and in the United Kingdom (UK), and destined, well already citizens of the Kingdom of Heaven; this uniqueness may be seen in our devotionals as you read and come across both USA and UK terminology or wordings. Enjoy!

Testimonials

Spring Forth is truly a powerful, yet simply written devotional that possesses the ability to speak to the seasoned Jesus follower, as well as those who are simply curious, or starting their journey of faith. Spring Forth fills a gap that many devotionals have often missed. This devotional is practical, with each devotional piece, not only inspiring, but also compelling and challenging the reader to take action, based on the powerful, bible-based insights shared.

The insightful thoughts shared on the pages of Spring Forth speaks life to the reader, and acts as a breath of fresh air - giving a gentle breeze to the sail, as we navigate the ups and down, twists and turns of life.

Disclaimer, the pages of this devotional will cause you to trust God at a whole new level, as it magnifies Who God is in your life, as well as assuring you of God's constant love towards you, His presence and the availability of His unquenchable grace.

Spring Forth is a 'get up and press on' type of devotional, helping you as the reader to get a deeper understanding of the seasons you might find yourself, whilst helping you to fix your eyes on the purpose of each season.

Spring Forth unveils biblical truth in an everyday linguistic and relevant manner; dispensing hope to those who might be lost or over-whelmed by life. The hope that is littered all over the pages of this devotional, from 'The Potter's Process' to 'Hiding The Word' will lift you up and realign you back to your rightful place, with a posture of worship, surrender and unrelenting trust in our Saviour.

Pastor Gbenga Ajewole
Lead Pastor, The Rock Church London Mission

Spring Forth is more than a devotional; it is a spiritual kit for effective living and transformation into God's original intention for us.

Olaniyi Ayeni
Founder Codespark Foundation,
Co-founder Capacity Development Group

Full of godly motivation and bursting with scripture, Spring Forth is a breath of fresh air and just what the doctor (the great Physician Himself) ordered.

Tose Umobuarie
Singer/Songwriter

Spring Forth is a devotional for everyone no matter what stage you are in your journey. It will motivate you, inspire you, teach you and refresh you.

Eloho Jocelyn Efemuai
Heartsong Ministries

Spring Forth is one of those books that is like fresh manna from heaven. The book is masterfully and beautifully written, full of wise counsel, filled with life-changing applications and is simply a blessing to read. This book is carefully constructed through diligent meditation and instruction from God's Holy Word that will enable every reader to take hold of powerful kingdom truths.

Daniel Babalola
Informed 2 Transformed Ministry

This is a rich compilation of divine truth that will encourage and empower to lead to a deeper intimacy with God.

Pastor Ruth Mateola
Associate Pastor, Kingdom Faith Ministries, Milton Keynes UK

I love how the authors infused some of their own personal life stories and experiences into the Spring Forth devotional, which makes the reading interesting and the points well communicated, after all, who doesn't like a good story. Did I mention that the name is prophetic as well? Yes! I believe every single lesson in this book will do just what the name implies; it will cause you to spring forth!

Joy Lifechangers
Life Coach

Table of Contents

Foreword..iv

Introduction v

Testimonials...vii

Spring

....11

1. God, My Strength 12
2. Come Alive 14
3. Now is the Time 16
4. The Overflow.. 19
5. The Great Healer 21
6. Choose Today... 23
7. Mold Me 24
8. The Potter's Process/Plan................................. 26
10. Rejection 31
11. Confidence in Christ....................................... 33
12. No More Condemnation 35
13. Choose Wisely.. 37
14. My Help.. 38
15. Beauty Beyond the Box 40
16. Joy Over Jericho 42
17. Christ-Like Character...................................... 44
18. Change the Game 45
19. Silence.. 46
20. Wisdom from Above....................................... 48

Forward

....51

1. What's Love Got To Do With It? 52
2. It's All About You Jesus! 54
3. Ceaseless Prayer.. 56

4. Jesus, Where Are You?..58

5. Hiding the Word..60

6. Heavenly Wealth...62

8. Are You A Thornbush?..66

9. Who Do You Look Like? 69

10. The Cup 72

11. Procrastination Playground 74

12. First Love...78

13. The Power of Passion..82

14. Follow-Follow...85

15. Compromised Intimacy...89

16. The Presence of God 91

17. Praying with Purpose 93

18. Trusting Love 96

19. The Possibility of Holiness...98

20. In His Image..100

Emerge

.... 103

1. To Worship You I Live 104

2. The Radiance of God..106

3. Outliving The Flesh...108

4. Righteousness a Gift! 110

5. The Mind is a Battlefield..112

6. The Power of Sharing...114

7. The Mask 116

8. New Season Shift...118

9. Worthy 120

10. The Reflection in the Mirror..122

Spring Forth Devotional Checklist...124

Spring

~ Mercy ~

1. God, My Strength

*"But the Lord is faithful; he will strengthen you
and guard you from the evil one."*

2 Thessalonians 3:3 NLT

Have you ever found yourself in a situation where it is difficult to keep your head above water? I'm not speaking of the pool, beach, or ocean; I'm talking about challenges of life. We get to points in life where we say things like - "I just can't make it." A good example of such a situation is a woman in her 30s who dates tirelessly in attempts to find the right guy. She puts her heart into every relationship but continues to be defeated. Does this describe you? Another example is a young man who works so hard to get a promotion but at every possibility of a promotion, it slips right through his fingers – Is that person you? We experience so much in life that we get to the point of giving up, and inevitably, some do. We exhaust all our efforts but fail, and the next sentence out of our mouths usually is - "Why me?"

Our friend, Job, in the Bible is a perfect example. He was a man who walked diligently with God, so much that God Himself, boasted about Him. The devil decided to tempt Job and took all that belonged to Him. Job couldn't keep his head above the water. He lost all his children and everything he had worked hard for; he felt like he couldn't make it anymore. "Why me?" was the question that continuously crossed his mind. Why would God take my children, my wife, my cattle, and my home? Why me?

Are you asking the same questions right now?

Why would you allow me to be unhappy? Why would You allow them to demote me at work? Why would You allow me to be diagnosed with a terminal illness? Why would You allow people to mock me? Why would You allow me to be stuck in this wheelchair? Why? Why? Why?

Though it looks really bad right now, you can't give up because when you find yourself in such situations in life, you are at the point of a BREAKTHROUGH! This is when God arises to take control. You see, God cannot fully drive the car when you still have your hands on the steering wheel. You have to let go of the steering wheel and allow God to drive you into your destiny. Trust me, He has mastered your car; so, give Him the wheel; He is faithful and will not fail!

Action Point - Prayers:

Take some time to read through and pray the following prayer points:

1. Faithful God, Your abundant grace is sufficient for me.[1] Through Your grace, I have hope and, in my hope, I am reminded of Your faithfulness. Lord, allow Your grace to always flow through me.

---

[1] 2 Corinthians 12:9

2. Many are the afflictions of the righteous but because of Your faithfulness, You O Lord, deliver me from them all. Deliver me today Lord.[2]

3. I am broken Lord; I have lost all hope. Rekindle Your fire in me and let Your faithfulness fight for me.

4. I know that You are the Ocean Divider, Lord divide every spirit of doubt in me. Do not allow them to overwhelm me again. I rebuke and dismantle every thought that I can't make it, separate these thoughts from me in Jesus name.

---

[2] Psalm 34:19

2. Come Alive

"So, I spoke this message, just as he told me. Suddenly as I spoke, there was a rattling noise all across the valley. The bones of each body came together and attached themselves as complete skeletons. Then as I watched, muscles and flesh formed over the bones. Then skin formed to cover their bodies, but they still had no breath in them. So, I spoke the message as he commanded me, and breath came into their bodies. They all came to life and stood up on their feet—a great army"

Ezekiel 37:7,10 NLT

Anyone that has planted a seed understands that the process is not completed in a day; the process requires patience and care. After the seed has been planted, you can't just leave it there and expect it to spring forth. No! You must actively work towards the growth of that seed. The same requirements are necessary for your spiritual, financial, and emotional life.

Let's take a young lady that wants to lose weight for example. She must first decide in her heart that she wants to lose weight and must then work on her decision. This requires exercise, a healthy lifestyle, and continuous monitoring of her health. The moment she decides to ignore the necessary interventions, she leaves room for cheat days, and then the cheat days will grow into cheat weeks. By the time she knows it, she's back where she started.

Your spiritual life is no different; you must constantly groom your spirit so that it does not become weak. You must always nourish and water your spirit so that it blossoms and grows into a large garden that will benefit all who gaze upon or pluck from it. Remember now that anything that you put into your system is what waters your garden. Music, friends, social media, TV, where you go, what you do, and who you surround yourself with all impact your spirit. How do you water your garden? The WORD of God is key and it is what makes your spirit come alive and stay alive. Are you watering your garden? When you starve your spirit, you are actually killing the power that God has given to you; you are destroying your destiny, which you cannot reach without your spirit being in agreement with you. The Word of God is the master key to unlock your destiny.

The Power in the Word

The words of the Bible are not old, dead words; they are *"...alive and active. Sharper than any double-edged sword, [these words] penetrate even to dividing soul and spirit, joints and marrow; it judges the thoughts and attitudes of the heart."*[3]

These words can bring to life all that has been dormant within you. They can bring the dead back to life - just as Jesus did with Lazarus. These words can mend the broken hearted and cause peace to calm the storms of your life. The requirements

---

[3] Hebrews 4:12 NLT

are obedience to the word of God and faith. Nothing can come alive in your life if you don't believe. You must trust in the One that created you. He loves a heart filled with faith. He reminds us in Hebrews 11:6 that without faith, it is impossible to please Him. So, put on your Armor of faith to raise every good thing that has died in your life. Now, I want you to pray that prayer with caution. You are to raise every *good* thing that has died. Make sure your heart is aligned with God's Living Word so that everything the devil has put to death in your life will rise and live again. Remember also that there are some things that God Himself has killed that should not live again. Therefore make sure you pray with wisdom.

Action Point - Activity:

Identify the tools that you have been using to water your garden and list them below. Then, list the tools that you can use to improve your spiritual life.

Now, work on it.

3. Now is the Time

"In the time of my favor I heard you, and in the day of salvation I helped you."
I tell you, now is the time of God's favor, now is the day of salvation."

2 Corinthians 6:2 NIV

Looking back over the past 12 months, an innumerable number of individuals have died for varying reasons. The young and old alike took their last breaths due to sickness, accidents, murders, and natural causes - the list goes on. As heart breaking as this is, it should also be a lesson to those of us who still have another chance by God's grace with each new day that we see.

As a wife, mother, sister, friend, mentor, and woman of God, I always endeavour to encourage as many people as I can to live ON purpose, live IN purpose, and to live WITH purpose because we are on earth for a mission. God has a calling for every one of us, but are we living *the purpose?* I have encountered so many people with amazing plans, goals, and dreams but nothing becomes of them; I'm almost certain that some die with their dreams. This must not be the case for you. God has placed GREATNESS within you and it is time to give birth. Stop the procrastination, rebuke the fear, and abort the excuses. Stop saying "I will start tomorrow" and push into purpose NOW!

Let us contrast life's challenges with the process of labour that takes a woman through a few stages before delivering a baby.

Stage One of Labour: Early Labour and Active Labour

The pregnant woman in this stage goes from contractions - which help the baby move through the canal - to early labour, and then active labour; this is the longest phase in the process of labour.

In this stage, she begins to feel stronger contractions that are not too far apart. Her water breaks and excruciating back pain occurs - the pain intensifies.

Stage One of Life: Endurance and Trial Phase

The rejections, pains, sufferings, heartaches, and problems that you have encountered thus far represent the contractions a pregnant woman has. Even though this is the longest process, giving up is not an option. There is no turning back at this point because you've been holding on to this vision for too long, and the only way out is forward.

In this phase, your faith is tested and tried in the fire. Shadrack, Meshach, and Abednego knew this phase just too well. Your faith may have been tested with the death of someone close, or homelessness; it may have been tested by a cheating spouse, lack of funds to treat a disease, a termination letter at work, a wayward child,

16

financial instability, a rejected proposal, an unsuccessful project, or a feeling of failure. But this feeling is only for a moment and it will be over in the twinkling of an eye.

Stage Two of Labour: Here Comes the Baby.

At this stage, the mother begins to push the baby out.

Stage Two of Life: The Push

You are now about to see what you have laboured for come to reality. You have worked hard and it is now time to see the product of your work. You have suffered long enough and it is now time to celebrate. Your contractions have lasted long enough. The tears have fallen for way too long; the sun is now rising. So, START PUSHING.

This is where you are right now; it's time to deliver the baby.

There are some things in you that you have wanted to pursue for years; the passion for your dreams burns within you like a wildfire! Your ideas are like the coals that you add to the fire but you are yet to reveal them to the world. Listen, the world awaits your greatness and the generations to come plead for your impact; they depend on it. Everyone anticipates the child's birth when a woman is in travail. If Thomas Edison did not give birth to the artificial light bulb, we may still be using lamps for light; we are benefitting from his invention. If Abraham did not take a leap of faith when he heard from God, he would never have been described as the Father of Nations. We are profiting from Abraham's obedience to the voice of God. You have been designed for such a time as this, and your case is not different; do not allow your existence to be void of purpose. God has already completed His work within you, all you must do is give birth to those amazing plans. You have been dreaming for too long. The moment to act is here, so wake up.

I don't know who you are, but the Lord has given me a word for you. You've been held down for too long, but God is stretching out His hand and calling your name. He wants you to trust Him and walk on water; He's telling you that you will not drown. He says; NOW IS THE TIME!

Action Point – Prayers & Declaration:

Take some time to read through and pray the following prayer points:

1. Amazing King of Glory, I thank You for waking me up from my sleep of slumber. Your love towards me is beyond words. I am grateful Lord that I am awake now and I can begin to walk in purpose. Today, I release the fire that I have enclosed within me into the world. Lord, let this fire burn for the world to see.'

' Ephesians 3:20

17

2. I declare with the Holy Spirit this day that I will not die with my dreams and goals! Lord, You have placed them within me and I must reveal them to the world. Give me the grace Lord to press forward and reveal Your glory to the world.[5]

3. Every fear, every spirit of failure: you power of procrastination, you demon of anxiety, you worrisome spirit, what are you doing within me? You only come to "steal, kill and destroy!"[6] Today, I deliver your eviction notice to you right now! You are no longer welcome here, leave right now in Jesus name.

Declaration: I am walking ON purpose, WITH purpose, and IN purpose. Give Birth Now!

---

[5] Ephesians 4:7
[6] John 10:10

4. The Overflow

"Listen to this message from the Lord! This is what the Lord says: By this time tomorrow in the markets of Samaria, six quarts of choice flour will cost only one piece of silver, and twelve quarts of barley grain will cost only one piece of silver."

2 Kings 7:1 NLT

I remember looking for a job some years ago; I did everything I could to find the perfect job. I searched high and low. I updated my resume to give it an official, authentic, and professional look. I emailed every company I could think of, and then I took my search beyond the walls of my home. I got off the couch and began hand delivering my CV to companies. I dressed up and walked into offices confidently with a smile on my face only to be rejected. The more effort I put in, the more the rejections came. I was experiencing a drought; it was a desert no one else could see or feel until the day the Lord spoke to me with 2 Kings 7. Right before that encounter, I had been fasting and soaking myself in worship. Though I was fed up, I decided to praise my way through. I had exhausted myself praying so much, but my prayers were about my wants and not about His desires for my life; even with my many tears, there were no results.

At some point, I was reminded that even if He did not do it, He would still be God, a perfect God at that. So, I decided not to stress about it any longer, I surrendered it all and praised Him just because HE IS GOD. That night, the Lord spoke to me and He said, "By this time tomorrow". I was taken to the book of 2 Kings 7: 3-11, where the lepers were at the point of death due to hunger. The Lord opened a door that they would not have ever imagined. He caused the Aramean army to literally go crazy! They began hearing things, panicked, and ran for safety – leaving everything behind.

The lepers were able to go into the camp where they ate, drank, took silver, gold, and so much more that they decided to go and tell the gatekeepers what happened. The overflow was beyond what they could handle, so they began to tell others of the Lord's blessings.

This word empowered me so much that I arose the next morning singing and dancing. Three hours later, a call came in from one of the companies that had previously rejected me and asked if I was still interested in the position. Apparently, a mistake had been made and they wanted to hire me; they not only hired me, I was given a position that was beyond my expectation, a position I wasn't even qualified for! Just like that, God did it.

I want to encourage and remind you today that God is still there for you, and His overflow is awaiting you. He's able to do exceedingly, abundantly, above all that you can think or ask. But you must trust Him, the process, and His greatness.

19

Action Point - Prayers:

Take some time to read through and pray the following prayer points:

1. Father, today I give it all to You. Things seem hard right now, I feel like I'm drowning in my troubles, but I give it all to You. You are my flotation device, and I know that You will not allow me to sink. You will keep me above water and cause me to land on shore safely.[7]

2. Dear Lord, I acknowledge that I have been selfish. I have selfishly placed my desires above Yours as if I know what is right for my life. I have exhausted all my efforts and realise that You have the key to my success. Therefore, today Lord, I give You permission to take my hand and lead me to the paths of righteousness and cause Your will to be done.[8]

3. My Saviour, You can do what no man can do! "You prepare a feast for me in the presence of my enemies. You [have] anointed my head with oil. My cup overflows!"[9] Father, let this overflow be so abundant that generations can drink from it.

4. Father, the enemy wants to have his way and torture me. He speaks false truths about the drought that precedes Your overflow! Father, cause my enemies to scatter at the sound of Your footsteps.[10] Disarm them! Let confusion arise in their camp and pour Your rain over this drought!

5. You know best Father! You are the author and illustrator of my life's journey. You are aware of every corner, mountain, and valley that may be before me. So, dear Lord, let my desires be Your desires and Your thoughts be my thoughts. Let my soul be aligned with You so that every thought that comes to my heart is ordered and directed by you.

6. Today, I declare that the drought in my life is over! My overflow has arrived! This overflow will be an overflow for me, my family, and generations to come.

Receive the rush of OVERFLOW right now!

---

[7] Psalm 69:14
[8] Psalm 25:5
[9] Psalm 23:5-6
[10] Psalm 68:1

5. The Great Healer

*"So Jesus and his disciples got up and went with him. Just then a woman
who had suffered for twelve years with constant bleeding came up behind him.
She touched the fringe of his robe, for she thought, "If I can just touch his robe,
I will be healed."*

Matthew 9:19-21 NLT

Remember the story of the woman with the issue of blood who touched the hem of Jesus' garment and was completely healed? What I love about this story is the power displayed. You see, Jesus was definitely capable of healing her but there's more to the story than this - there is power within us. In this scripture, we see the power of faith at work. Prior to this phase, she had lost all hope because she spent so much money on her disorder. I'm sure her friends and enemies even lead her astray in the name of healing. Before she got to this point, she had put her hope in man and trusted in the deliverance of man.

There are two things that we can learn from this story.

The Power Within Us

While Jesus healed the woman, the story would have been different without the woman's faith. We have to unleash the power of faith within us! We must be moved to act by faith; we must understand the power that is within us. Jesus said that we can do all things! Not some things, not a few things...NO! He said ALL things.[11] We have the power to command our troubles to flee. We have the power to command things to work in our favour according to HIS plan.

The Power of Faith

The scripture described the woman as one who had done everything possible but found no healing.[12] Thereafter, she believed! That was her weapon against her sickness: her belief! Your belief, your faith, can be your weapon too against the issue that makes you bleed every day. When she heard that Jesus would be passing through, she planned to touch him. She knew of the power flowing within and around Jesus and she refused to miss the opportunity to be healed. She knew that He would be able to restore her, and with all her faith she touched His cloak; she exhibited complete faith in Jesus.

Do you remember being in such a hopeless situation? I can confidently say that every single person reading this book has had an encounter where they believed in

---

[11] Philippians 4:13
[12] Mark 5:25-34

something or someone and were disappointed. Trusting in man leads to disappointment but trusting in God leads to everlasting joy. The Bible reminds us[13] that we cannot serve two masters; we cannot trust in man and trust in God. We must make a choice and that choice should be God! When you have faith in God, there is no need to spend hours on victory prayers. You say it, and it is done all because your faith is in God. Because we have *fled to Him for refuge [we] can have great confidence as we hold to the hope that lies before us. This hope is a strong and trustworthy ANCHOR for our souls. It leads us through the curtain into God's inner sanctuary.*[14] Hallelujah!

Paul reminds us[15]and we must declare that at the name of Jesus EVERY knee must bow and confess that Jesus is Lord. Let me break it down for you. At the arrival, the landing, or appearance of the NAME of Jesus, EVERY power, creature, human, cancer, drug addiction, mental illness, generational curse, heartache, homelessness, stronghold, poverty, barrenness, shame, unemployment, impotence, sadness, pain, frustration etc. MUST come under the submission of Jesus and be SILENT! They are no longer permitted to act and are IMMEDIATELY rendered useless. The power has been released today to heal and deliver you.

Sickness is not only physical; it is emotional, spiritual, and mental. With faith, I want you to do this: place your hand over the area that is causing you pain and repeat this prayer:

Action Point - Prayer:

Father, I pray for healing right now in the name of Jesus. Submerge me in the blood of the Lamb so that I am restored. I replace my blood with the blood of Jesus. I bear the mark of Jesus upon me and I command every pain I feel to leave now in Jesus name.

Feeling restored yet? Claim your healing INSTANTLY.

---

[13] Matthew 6:24
[14] Hebrew. 6:18
[15] Philippians 2:10

6. Choose Today

"...then choose today whom you will serve. Would you prefer the gods your ancestors served beyond the Euphrates? Or will it be the gods of the Amorites in whose land you now live? But as for me and my family, we will serve the Lord."

Joshua 24:15 NLT

Let's take a trip back to the Garden of Eden. Remember how Eve, who was created to complete Adam, chose to heed to the voice of Satan? She made a choice to eat from the forbidden fruit.

God loves us so much that He gave us the opportunity to choose because He doesn't want forced love; He wants genuine love. He worked so hard to prove His love and that love should be enough for us to choose Him every single time. When we refuse to be angry, we choose Him. When we deny Satan, we choose Him. When we allow ourselves to be persecuted by the world for his sake, we choose Him. When we cry out to Him in pain, we choose Him. Choosing God is your way of telling Him, Father, I am yours, always and forever. Rain or shine, sleet or snow, I choose You.

This should be our constant declaration. You may be asking yourself why it is necessary to continuously speak these words; the answer is simple. As we transit through life, our thoughts, actions, character, cultures, and environments cause us to fall short of His glory, because of this, we must die to our flesh daily (1 Corinthians 15:31) and remind ourselves who we are in Christ. We must also remind Satan that we are children of God. Satan will always try to discredit us after God has validated us, so we must stand firm in our decisions to choose Him. Most importantly, we must show God that we are still a part of His army, a citizen of His kingdom.

Joshua made this decision when he said "But if you refuse to serve the Lord, then choose today whom you will serve. Would you prefer the gods your ancestors served beyond the Euphrates? Or will it be the gods of the Amorites in whose land you now live? But as for me and my family, we will serve the Lord."[16]

Make your decision today!

Action Point - Prayer:

Dear Lord, I know I have gone astray several times but today, I repent and stand on top of the highest mountain to declare that I am Yours.

Omnipotent, it is so comforting in your arms; I want to stay in this place forever. Being in Your secret place and under Your shadow is my insurance. Therefore, I declare that as for me and my house, we will serve the Lord. Amen.

---

[16] Joshua 24:15

7. Mold Me

And yet, O LORD, You are our Father.
We are the clay, and You are the Potter.
We all are formed by Your hand.

Isaiah 64:8 NLT

I fall short of words as I attempt to describe the relationship between the Potter and the clay. The love that the Potter has for the clay is beyond words. The obedience that the clay must succumb to is phenomenal. Without words, the two express themselves through emotions, beauty, and skill. They speak to one another without utterances, but just like the sky, their messages spread throughout all the earth.[17] When I imagine the setting, I see a silent room with a chair for the Potter and a pile of clay; no one is permitted to enter. The colours of the wall had been painted light brown in order to eliminate distractions and create an atmosphere for utmost concentration in which the Potter can create His unique piece. Once the Potter closes the door, footsteps within the foyer are forbidden for this is the course of formation.

Let's go back for a moment. Before the Potter enters the Room of Creation, He goes through a process. He sets time apart to imagine, compose, implement, and evaluate His upcoming work of art. As He sits in silence, love fills His heart so much that it floods the entire palace. Every object, including the clay to be used in the other room, begins to drown in His love. Tears fill His eyes as He imagines what will become of His creation. Are they tears of joy or despair? Nevertheless, His love continues to flow. Even the trees bow upon exposure to this great love. Rain freezes at the entrance of His love. What a great love it is!

Now, back to the Room of Creation. The Potter carefully searches for the perfect pile of clay to use. Once He has identified it, Operation Creation begins. He holds the piece in His hands and stares at it. Even the glare in His eyes possesses love. A tear drops from His eye onto the centre of the clay and He knows right there, in that moment, that He has found the perfect piece. He places the clay in the centre of the wheel and begins to work. The clay is rebellious at first and attempts to be disobedient but the Potter does not give up. With love, He presses it against the centre of the wheel as it spins in place. The Potter never takes His eyes off the clay. He smoothens every jagged edge, bump, and crack and works on His piece until it is perfect. Within perfection He adds His very nature, He shapes the inner core of His masterpiece to be JUST LIKE HIM.

During the whole process, He does not breathe, as His breath signifies completion. At the point of completion, He lets out His breath and the sound of the harp is

---

[17] Psalm 19:3

released. Music fills the mansion and He smiles with joy. He looks at His work and He sees that His creation is good.

The masterpiece is then transported to the wilderness to become all that it has been created to be. During its journey, the clay picks dust and dirt, it feels anger and pain, and it experiences trouble and hardship, but the Potter never takes His eyes off His masterpiece. The clay breaks and immediately, the Potter picks up the broken pieces and returns to the Room of Creation. He places the clay back onto the spinning wheel and begins to remold, reshape, restore, and repair it; the pain in His heart pours out as love and the whole process begins again - you are the clay in the hands of the Potter.

Action Point - Prayers:

Take some time to read through and pray the following prayer points:

1. Oh! How I love You Lord, for Your love for me engulfs the world. You made and formed me into perfection, and I am grateful. Thank You Lord for loving me so dearly.

2. Master, just as Your love reflects for me to see, help me to love You more each day. Help me to always choose You over the things of this world and help me to seek the things of heaven first.

3. I have been broken Lord. I did not keep my eyes on You, so I fell into temptation. I am sorry Lord, and I plead for Your forgiveness. Remember that the blood that flows through me is not blood but Your love. Soak and wash me in Your laundry, Father, until I am as white as snow.[18]

4. In obedience Lord, I succumb to Your original formation. I have taken a detour on this journey, but I am now back on track. Help me Lord as I lift up my eyes unto the hills.[19]

5. My Architect, remember our conversation in the Room of Creation. Remember the tear that fell from Your eye when You held me in Your hands and reconstructed my broken pieces. Remember me today O Lord and hear my cry.

---

[18] Psalm 51:7 MSG
[19] Psalm 121

8. The Potter's Process/Plan

"...Like clay in the hand of the potter, so are you in my hand"

Jeremiah 18:6 NIV

As joy overwhelms the Potter at His upcoming creation, He transforms into the Alpha (the Beginning). He sits at the drawing board and begins to map out His creation; no detail is left out. He imagines what glory He wants to put into this masterpiece. He considers the greatness that will become of it. Every step is written down, every step is ordered. His words within His heart are so loud that without opening His mouth they pour forth. He will be conceived on this day. His mother will feel his first kick at 3:52 am and she will go into labour at 7:21 am. The labour will be challenging only because the entrance of greatness is never easy. She will bear him and he will let out his first cry at 9:26 pm. He will weigh 7lbs and 4oz and his length will be 19 inches. The excited Potter smiles at the thought of his mother's joy as He continues to map out His plans for the boy's life. As I continue to watch the Potter, I notice His countenance shift often, and I wonder why. Every time His countenance changed, I noticed the map had a dark path, and right after the dark path, there was a crown! But what did the dark paths mean? I continued to watch.

The Potter spoke to the clay, "Listen, my precious masterpiece. I want you to know that you are a chosen person, part of a royal priesthood and a holy nation; you are My very own possession"[20], "I don't want you to forget – I formed your inward parts, I knitted you together in your mother's womb, you are fearfully and wonderfully made"[21], "I know the plans I have for you, they are plans of good and not of evil, to give you an expected end"[22], "You have been anointed to preach good tidings to the meek, to bind up the broken hearted, to proclaim liberty to the captives and to open the prison to them that are bound".[23]

However, it will not be an easy journey my love; Satan will attack you; he will send principalities in the form of friends, family, anger, cancer, poverty, deception, failure, and even death to those you love, but do not be dismayed. I want you to understand that the enemy will strike your heel, but you will always crush his head.[24]Despite all these things, overwhelming victory is yours through Christ, who will always love you.[25] But always remember to submit yourself to me. Resist the devil and he will flee from you.[26] Never give up! Remember that the temptations in your life are no different from what others experience. I will never allow the temptation

---

[20] 1 Peter 2:9
[21] Psalm 139: 13-14
[22] Jeremiah. 29:11
[23] Isaiah 61:1
[24] Genesis 3:15
[25] Romans 8:37
[26] James 4:7

to be more than you can stand. When you are tempted, I will show you a way out so that you can endure.[27] Remember today that I have armed you with strength for the battle. I have subdued your enemies under my feet. I have placed your foot on their necks. I have destroyed all who hated you. They even cried to me, but I refused to answer; I ground them as fine as dust in the wind. I have swept them into the gutter like dust. I have already given you victory over your accusers.[28] I have given you the power to push back the enemies; use my name to trample on your foes.[29]

But trust my process:

- When you don't have money to pay your rent – Trust the Process.
- When your father/mother disowns you – Trust the Process.
- When you have that miscarriage – Trust the Process.
- When you go for a check-up and the doctor tells you that you have cancer – Trust the Process.
- When you cry all night, and want to give up – Trust the Process.
- When you fail that exam – Trust the Process.
- When your friends hate you for no reason – Trust the Process.
- When the enemies seem to be greater than the friends – Trust the Process.
- When you are told that you will amount to nothing – Trust the Process.
- When your best friend dies and you have no one left – Trust the Process.

I realised that those dark paths were the troubles that the young boy would have to endure. It saddened the Potter because He knew that it would be a trying time for the young lad. However, the Potter was filled with joy by each crown that He placed after the dark paths; it all made sense. The crowns represented promotion, elevation, success, happiness, favour, grace, mercy, and joy, while the dark paths were set in place as trials. In order to receive a crown, the young lad had to persevere through a dark alley. The dark path was sickness, deception, frustration, failure and all the negative things that one could possibly think of. But the Potter was confident that no matter how hard the obstacles were, His clay would succeed.

After prophesying unto the clay, He sealed up the area He spoke into, transformed into the Omega (the End), and molded the clay with His hands. He proceeded to the wheel and began to work as Elohim (the Creator).

---

[27] 1 Corinthians 10:13
[28] Psalm 18:39-43
[29] Psalm 44:5

Action Point - Meditation:

I want you to remember today that God is aware of everything that you are going through. He planned it all, just to make you great! Hang in there! Your crown awaits you.

9. The Latter Rain

Oh, that we might know the Lord! Let us press on to know Him. He will respond to us as surely as the arrival of dawn or the coming of rains in early spring.

Hosea 6:3 NLT

Growing up as a child in England, I was always enthusiastic about the rain. Whenever it rained, my siblings and I would put on our rain boots, go outside and jump in the puddles made by the rain. My rain boots were yellow and I had a matching raincoat; I was always excited to put them on. For some reason, I found peace in the splashing of water. I didn't think of anything else other than the rain falling on my face.

A man with an interview scheduled to start in 45 minutes may find the rain inconvenient, especially when he forgot his umbrella on the countertop; did I mention he is running late for the interview? The mother who has to walk home with her kids in the rain may also find rain inconvenient. And even those who are not graced to have a home would cry at the thought of heavy rainfall. But God is a God with purpose; knowing God is a step closer to understanding why He does the things He does.

There are times when we want rain, or a specific blessing, or we need God to answer a specific prayer but we don't receive an answer, at those times, is God silent? When we are in desperate need of something that will help us live better lives and even grow in purpose but we hear *"No"*, at those times, is He being mean? Does He hate us?

Of course, not!

God is a God of time, purpose, and position. He always works with correct timing, for the correct purpose, and in the correct position. No matter when the rain falls, trust God because He is the Master Planner working it all out; He makes all things beautiful in His time.

Exploring rain a little more reveals it can be compared to the season of harvest. As you may know, people (especially subsistence farmers) usually plant crops around October or November with the hopes of harvesting around March or April. They know they need to plant on *time* with the *purpose* of producing crops, which must be in the correct *position* where moisture, rain, and sun will help the crops grow.

You see my friend; rain also represents God's provision. He meets our needs through the rain. And when the rain finally pours, you feel relief as you see your hard work begin to spring forth. If you don't believe me, ask someone in a dry land who has barely had rainfall. When the rain finally comes, everyone is happy, you even see children running outside in the rain to play; to them it is a sign of relief.

The little girl who has finally been graced to see and feel the rain after being confined to a hospital bed can also testify to what I am saying; for her it is a sign of happiness. The fruit stand owner who has a sales plan for the coming months also understands the purpose of rain.

Now what does this mean to you?

It means that your latter rain is not delayed, it will come on time but you must not stop planting. You must continue to work hard and strive for what you want and at the appointed time, He will send the rain. I'm not talking about a rain of destruction; I'm speaking of the rain of purpose, position, and time. He will send an answer to your prayers. He will speak a word of hope into your life, and complete what He has started.

Don't get distracted by the rain on the windshield or your wet clothes after running in the rain, realise that He is working on your harvest and very soon you will be like the little child laughing, singing, and splashing in the rain.

Action Point - Prayer:

Dear Lord, help me to see beyond the clouds and other elements to see the purpose in the rain. Help me to appreciate that You are completely in control of the seasons, not just of the universe but also of my life. Help me to trust in Your timing, Your purpose and Your positioning for my life – because only when these are aligned with You will all things work together for my good and I will reap the reward of the latter rain. Thank You Lord Jesus.

10. Rejection

The Lord said to Abraham after Lot had parted from him, "Look around from where you are, to the north and south, to the east and west. All the land that you see I will give to you and your offspring forever. I will make your offspring like the dust of the earth, so that if anyone could count the dust, then your offspring could be counted. Go, walk through the length and breadth of the land, for I am giving it to you."

Genesis 13:14-17 NIV

We all know too well what it feels like to be rejected, and I can confidently say that you have been through rejection at some point in time or maybe you are currently experiencing some form of rejection as you read this devotional. However, how we respond to rejection is what makes a difference.

There's nothing like loving someone with your whole heart, pouring all your efforts into building such a relationship and then helplessly watching it all go down the drain. Ask God, He knows all too well.

Your heart feels as if someone tore a piece out of your chest and you feel pain with every heartbeat. It may feel like an emotional rollercoaster. You experience feelings from: *"I want to hug you and tell you I love you"*, to *"I just want to be as far away from you as possible"*, You find yourself in an emotional turmoil that only you can understand. You want to explain it to someone else, but they just don't get it.

You were so positive that this person would be in your life and everything would just be great; you were so positive that this person wasn't just for a season, and then God intervened.

Here is what you need to understand:

- God is a jealous God and He will not share His glory with anyone. When God sees that you have placed someone else in His position, He will come between such a relationship, even if that means separating the two of you by any means possible.

- Rejection is necessary as it is a reminder of the contrast between the nature of mankind and that of God. God is perfect, not man, and you cannot serve two masters. You will love one and hate the other. God knows only too well what we need and therefore may allow separation even in relationships.

- Separation is needed for progress. Think about it. Abraham couldn't reach his potential that God designed for him until he separated from Lot;

- Friends can become enemies; it's not all friends that remain friends. It is quite easy for a friend to become envious of your success and then begin to hate you!

So, what's my point?

Give thanks to God for the rejection that you have experienced or the one that you are currently experiencing because He is making you stronger and wiser.

Listen:

- The fact that man rejected you doesn't mean that there is no way. God will pave a way for you because you are His child - man may reject you but God will never reject you.

- Some may have thought you were not good enough, so they overlooked you. They chose other candidates for the position you deserved, but now they are begging you to come and take your rightful position. God will ensure that you are not rejected from the place where He has placed you.

Action Point - Prayer:

Father, help me realise that everything that I encounter in life has been structured or allowed by You. You are perfect in all Your ways, in all that You do, and You make no mistakes.

11. Confidence in Christ

*Some trust in chariots, and some in horses: but we will remember the name
of the Lord our God. They are brought down and fallen: but we are risen,
and stand upright.*

Psalm 20:7 KJV

Allowing others to define you only results in self-limitation and disappointment.
Men cannot appreciate what they didn't create, at least not like the Creator Himself.
No matter how much you try, they will still see flaws and you will continue to try and
live up to their standards. The funny thing is, the standards that you try to live by
might not even have been achieved by those who judge you. They find flaws in you
because somewhere deep down within them they are hurt and broken. They love
what they see in you, so they despise you. This is not intentional behaviour; it is just
the state of the heart. Jeremiah 17:9 (NLT) tells us that:

*"The human heart is the most deceitful of all things, and desperately wicked. Who
really knows how bad it is?"*

So, when thinking about who you are or how great you can become, don't allow
man's deceitful heart to deceive you; allow God to analyse your life and define
you. No wonder David said that "Those who know your name trust in you, for you,
Lord, have never forsaken those who seek you".[30] David understood that trusting in
man was worthless and stated that we should run to the Lord for refuge instead of
putting our trust in man.[31] Now you know that for David to understand this principle
only meant one thing, he had tried and tested men, he had been through hell and
back with men – Saul springs to mind. He had been disappointed on numerous
occasions and so, in this Psalm we are forewarned. I wouldn't be surprised if at some
stage in his life, he searched for satisfaction from man and eventually realised that
his so-called friends could not provide what he sought.

Have you ever put your confidence in man? Have you been disappointed? Have
you been hurt, troubled, or betrayed? God has a word for you; He is telling you
right now: "Trust Me! I will never leave nor disappoint you. Trust me and lean not
on your own understanding".[32]

Allow God to be your confidence today.

---

[30] Psalm 9:10
[31] Psalm 118:8
[32] Proverbs 3:5

Action Point - Activity:

Examine the past few months and see how many times you have allowed others to define you. How did it make you feel? How did you respond thereafter? Say no to the interpretation of man today, and yes to your true definition which is in Christ Jesus. The Bible says: "It's in Christ that we find out who we are and what we are living for".[33]

List down areas in your life that you have allowed others to define you. Pray about these insecurities and take back your identity.

----

[33] Ephesians 1:11 (MSG)

12. No More Condemnation

There is therefore now no condemnation to them which are in Christ Jesus,
who walk not after the flesh, but after the Spirit.

Romans 8:1 KJV

We tend to try to predict God and His feelings towards us. We assume that He is angry with us or is punishing us for our sins. Whenever we go through struggles, our first thought is usually "I must have done something to deserve this; God is punishing me for my behaviour", but the truth is that if God was to truly punish us for our behaviour, we would not be alive. Our sins deserve death but His love and His compassion reveal mercy.

We must realise that we cannot understand how God thinks because "His thoughts are not our thoughts, neither are His ways our ways".[34] We cannot continue to live as slaves when we are sons and daughters of God. He doesn't look at our sins but He considers His love towards us. Nevertheless, we cannot continue to live in sin and expect grace to abound.[35] There must be a change of heart and a consequent departure from the wayward life; drinking, smoking, fighting, bullying, malice, adultery, fornication, lying, stealing, gossiping, and the likes, as these are all hindrances to our purpose and experiencing eternal glory.

God wants a change today.

"Let them be a living and holy sacrifice—the kind he will find acceptable. This is truly the way to worship him. Don't copy the behaviour and customs of this world, but let God transform you into a new person by changing the way you think. Then you will learn to know God's will for you, which is good and pleasing and perfect."[36]

What lifestyle do you possess that is a hindrance to your eternal glory? What are you doing that can be an obstacle to experiencing His glory? God cannot exist where there is filth, but He is able to cleanse you and make a way for you to come out from a life of sin; O yes, He will help you by the Holy Spirit and His transforming Word (Jesus) but ultimately, the decision to act and to change is yours to make.

Is the worldly accolades you are currently experiencing worth separation from God? It's funny how we want to live and have all the *ungodly* fun that the world has to offer and then expect to be a partaker of His eternal kingdom. If you didn't want Him on earth, why would you want Him thereafter? The choices you make now will determine the consequences of life after this world is over.

---

[34] Isaiah 55:8
[35] Romans 6:1
[36] Romans 12:1-2

It's not too late now to create a solid relationship with Him. Allow Him to be first in your life. Discover the promises and purpose that He has for you. Eliminate the distractions, align your heart with Him, and you will see that His desires will be your desires and His thoughts for your life will be in sync with yours. Ask Him to order your steps.[37]

"Come close to God, and God will come close to you. Wash your hands, you sinners; purify your hearts, for your loyalty is divided between God and the world."[38]

"So you must live as God's obedient children. Don't slip back into your old ways of living to satisfy your own desires. You didn't know any better then. But now you must be holy in everything you do, just as God who chose you is holy. For the Scriptures say, "You must be holy because I am holy."[39]

When you hand your life over to Christ. When you live for Him, there may be conviction of sin but there is no certainly no condemnation!

Action Point - Prayer:

Thank You Father for Your unfailing love. Today I commit my life to You. I surrender my whole life and heart to You. Use me as You please Lord. Amen.

---

[37] Psalm 119:133
[38] James 4:8
[39] 1 Peter 1:14-16 NLT

13. Choose Wisely

For God, who said, "Let there be light in the darkness," has made this light shine in our hearts so we could know the glory of God that is seen in the face of Jesus Christ.

2 Corinthians 4:6 NLT

Being consumed with the things of the world can cause us to make a lot of mistakes. The world that we live in right now is so self-centred. Unfortunately, we have allowed the world to define who we are. People are so consumed with *selfies, fashion, likes* and *shares*. People base their importance on how many times their pictures are liked on Facebook, Instagram, or Twitter so much so that not getting the likes they want may lead to depression; they see themselves as worthless and inferior, and begin to compare themselves to the next person who has 5 million likes.

You see, the thing is – they seek definition from the world. They choose to base their self-worth on the opinions of others. Why give them permission to decide how valuable you are? Why aren't our desires on the One who created and formed us from our mother's wombs?

Psalm 139 gives a vivid description of the love of God and His work of creation. He intimately took His time to create us – uniquely. He made our inner parts, and even His thoughts about us are precious. More precious than anything man can tell. Therefore, our desires should be to have HIS approval, which is the only approval that matters.

We cannot continue to live selfishly. We must remember that it is not about us, but about God. He owns us; everything that we think belongs to us actually belongs to Him - He gave all that we have to us, so the praises are not ours but His. We should not be engulfed in self-love and self-promotion, but in His eternal love for us, and promotion of His glory. His love is so great that He gave us His only Son. He allowed him to leave his position of eternal glory and placed him into a treacherous world to be tortured, bruised, and crucified just to reveal how much He loves you and I.[40]

Let's forget about vain glory, rather let's praise and surrender all glory unto whom it belongs.

Action Point - Prayer:

Father, help me to stay focused on You. Teach me to be selfless and committed to You all the days of my life. Do not allow me to be consumed by the distractions of the world in Jesus Mighty Name. Amen.

---

[40] John 3:16

14. My Help

God is within her, she will not fall;
God will help her at break of day.

Psalm 46:5 NIV

Through the easy and tough times, I've identified the key to some treasures in life. There are so many that I don't think it's possible to identify them all. Think about it; the person who owns all the treasures is endless, so it would make sense that even His mysteries are infinite. As I continue to seek and grow in God, I am introduced to a new vision of who He is and what He can do; I am also introduced to a new me.

I remember growing up and one of the statements that I constantly saud was "You don't know me". It's funny because when I said it, I believed that I knew myself. However, the truth was that I was a visitor to myself. I was confused and had no clue about who I truly was. I thought I knew who God had created me to be in life but the truth is I had no idea; I really didn't know. I now understand that I have no identity outside of Christ. I am nothing without Him. He makes me who I am. I have an identity in Christ, and because of Christ I am free to soar like the eagles. I can walk freely without feeling condemned by what anyone has to say about me. I now understand what Paul meant when he said there is now no condemnation for those who are in Christ Jesus.41 It's simple: Christ equals freedom, however that freedom only pertains to those who have Christ, to those who desire to dine with Him, to be intimate with Him and to those who allow Him to order their steps.

So, I told you about being introduced to the *new me*, right? It sounds comical but it's true. I realised that life with Christ is completely different from life without Him. You can't just mingle with uncleanliness and feel free. No! The Holy Spirit is always at work convicting you. He is always reminding you to get back in line with who you truly are in Christ. No wonder James 4:4 stresses on making a choice between the world and God. For you cannot be a friend of the world and a friend of God. For a friend of the world is an enemy of God and a friend of God is an enemy of the world because the two will never mix. Remember you can't serve two masters.42 It's the same feeling for all those who choose to experience a life with Christ.

With the Holy Spirit at work within you, you will find that you yearn for things that nourish your soul and refrain from those behaviours that make you feel spiritually constrained. You avoid gatherings that are ungodly and you rejoice in experiences that bring you closer to your Maker.

The beauty in all this is that as you continue to grow in God, He allows you to grow in all things. He occupies your territory and possesses all that you desire.43 He holds you up so that you will not fall. He gives you courage in times of need and fills you

---

41 Romans 8:1
42 Matthew 6:24
43 Matthew 6:33

38

up so that you never thirst. He holds you up when the devil tries to knock you down. He stands as a mighty man in battle with you." You can be rest assured in the storm that He will cause peace even in chaos because He is the Peace Maker. You are guaranteed victory because He is the Mighty Man in Battle that separates you from catastrophe and consumes the enemy.

What an assurance we have in Jesus!

Thank You Jesus, my help comes from You.

Action Point - Meditation:

- Ponder on these words for a moment.

- Are you a friend of the world or a friend of God?

- Allow God to occupy your territory today and receive true freedom!

- Now thank God for being your constant help.

" Psalm 24:8

15. Beauty Beyond the Box

You will increase my greatness and comfort me again

Psalm 71:21 ESV

I want to encourage you today to experience the beauty beyond the box. I'm sure you're wondering what I'm talking about. "What is beauty beyond the box?"

Beauty beyond the box is experiencing something outside of your comfort zone. I encourage you today to step out of the box that you've been stuck in for quite a while. It may seem a little bit scary but trust me, it's beautiful beyond that box. You see there is greatness inside of you, but you need to reach outside of that box to experience the grandeur that God has in store for you.

Now it's not going to be easy. You might fall a couple of times and you might make some mistakes, but it's alright because those errors and falls make you stronger and they help you get up and do it better. Don't be afraid to fall; don't be afraid to trip. Go ahead and go beyond that box, you'll find beauty awaits you there.

Once I was seeing patients in the office, I looked out the window and noticed that the sky was dull. The clouds were out, but the sun was nowhere to be found. When the patients came in, the first thing they spoke about was the weather, it was cold, and the rain wouldn't let up. The rain soon stopped but as soon as I left work, it started raining again. The rain then turned into hail; five minutes later the hail stopped, and the sun suddenly appeared! It was so bright that I had to use the sun visor to shield my eyes while I was driving.

Let me tell you, my friend, there will be moments in life when it's going to be dull and when it will rain, there will even be days when it will start to hail. It may seem as if the whole world is against you; it may look as if it will never work out and you will feel like you want to give up. However, after that process, after that little season, the sun will come out, and it will be so beautiful all over again that everyone will want to be outside. You will begin to succeed again, and everything will start working in your favour AGAIN. So, don't worry about the dark times, focus on what's to come. Don't lock yourself inside; focus on what God has planned for you outside. Get out of that box that you've been in for so long and experience the beauty beyond the box as you let the sunshine on you.

It's great beyond the box; in fact, it's beautiful. Here's a little secret, the beauty beyond the box is waiting just for you, and no one else can have it. It is specific for your calling, vision, and purpose – so STEP OUT!!!!

I pray that the sun will shine brightly on you as you step outside the box. I pray that your faith will be increased such that you will continually step outside of self-imposed limits or those limitations that life has placed around you. I pray that as you build courage to get out of the box, God will push you into unimaginable success.

So, let me be the first to say – Congratulations on unveiling the beauty beyond the box.

Give God your hand and STEP out in faith!

Action Point - Activities:

In what areas of your life have you found it difficult to step out of the box? What impact has this had on your goals? In the first section below, list the things that you have been unable to do because you were afraid.

In the second section, list the steps you will take to achieve these goals. Make a decision to step outside the box, outside of your comfort zone today. Don't wait for tomorrow, start planning today.

Areas for improvement:

_____

_____

_____

_____

_____

_____

_____

_____

_____

Steps to achieve goals:

_____

_____

_____

_____

_____

_____

_____

_____

_____

16. Joy Over Jericho

"Shout! For the LORD has given you the city!"

Joshua 6:16 NIV

I can only imagine Joshua's nerves when He was given this major assignment. God basically asked him to load up on faith and march ahead without looking back. You can read the whole story in Judges 6.

Let's think about it for a second. This huge city had extremely large walls surrounding it, so large that even a bulldozer probably couldn't knock them down. The width and breadth were incredibly large that they had to devote seven days to walk around the city. They had to walk once a day around a city that God promised would be theirs. God didn't tell them to take large weapons with them, He didn't tell them to find the strongest men that would knock the walls down. No! God told Joshua to shout in order to knock the city down! Shout! Just shout! So, their voices were their weapons and the hallelujah proclamation their ammunition. Wow!

I am sure that you can relate to a situation in your life where God asked you to do something that you thought was really ridiculous. He may have asked you to move without telling you exactly where you are going. Friends, there are time where it looks like you might be defeated because you don't have the necessary skills needed for the battle ahead. God wants you to understand that if He did if for Joshua, He can surely do it for you.

To accomplish this major task that God gave to Joshua required faith, trust, and obedience. The shout represented victory. The shout was a prerequisite for victory. Their voices, faith, and obedience were their tools of victory.

The Lord makes the same request of you; He has a mission for you, as there are three walls of Jericho that you must destroy today.

Action Point - Activities:

The wall of obstacles preventing your purpose

- You have been destined to succeed. Your destiny says that just as the map of your life says it. You have already been pronounced a victor but Satan is not happy about it. He knows that once you become aware, and break the wall of obstacles preventing your purpose, he has lost the battle.

- Declare, plan, and act on your march today! Shout and receive your victory!

The wall of fear

- The greatest enemy of faith is fear. Fear causes stagnancy and separates us from what God can do in our lives; it is what the devil uses to tell us lies. We must fight the enemy called fear with faith! We must declare to fear that it no longer has occupancy in our territory because faith has taken over.

- Shout to the Lord today that you receive undeniable faith for the city has been given to you.

The wall preventing salvation

- This is the most important wall that you must break in life. Salvation has been given to all freely, but the lust of the world and the enticement that Satan constantly brings our way is the wall that prevents us from salvation. Every time that we give in to the world or the desires thereof, we continue to build a wall pushing us further away from salvation.

- The only way to break this wall is to focus on the things above. We must trust God and focus on our eternal salvation, for everything on earth is vanity; we must desire the things above.

Walk in faith, trust, and obedience. Shout to the Lord and receive your victory today!

17. Christ-Like Character

They also recognized them as men who had been with Jesus

Acts of Apostles 4:13 NLT

Declaring Christianity is not enough. I mean, let's be honest, murderers call themselves Christians, even Judas identified himself as a follower of Christ. Christianity is more than the words of the mouth; it is the lifestyle that we use our actions to preach.

In the scripture above, Peter and John were identified as men who were with Jesus. Can the same be said about you and I? Our lives must reflect our beliefs. Our behaviours must tell the story of whom we belong to. The words of our mouths must reflect our belief. It is necessary for us to stand out. There must be a difference between the world and us. Our existence alone must speak of His wonders. We cannot and must not conform to the world, but we must be transformed into who God has created us to be.[45]

If we truly want to spring forth, we must take a stand and stick by it. We cannot be of the Lord today and the world tomorrow. That is unacceptable! If we are luke-warm, He will spit us out[46] - this means complete rejection. Now we all know how it feels to be rejected by a friend or a loved one, but that is nothing compared to being rejected by the One who created you. I pray that we will not be rejected in Jesus name.

It is true that there are people that are in the world that make it without Christ, but their blessings are temporary, and what use is it to gain the whole world and lose your soul. We are not building our treasures on earthly soil or sand; we are building our heavenly home. We must understand the essence of storing up our treasures in heaven,[47] but we must truly be children of God in all that we do. Everything that we do must reflect Christ. People must be able to recognise that not only have we been with Jesus, but that we are always with him.

Action Point – Start Walking:

I want to dare you today to walk in Christ! Walk with Christ and ALWAYS walk for Christ! Get up now and start walking in the physical, prophetically declaring your walk with Christ in the spiritual.

---

[45] Romans 12:2
[46] Revelations 3:16
[47] Matthew 6:19-21

18. Change the Game

"But You, O Lord, shall endure forever, and the remembrance of Your name to all generations. You will arise and have mercy on Zion; for the time to favour her, yes, the set time, has come."

Psalm 102:12-13 NKJV

There's nothing like the waiting process, the silent chapter, the waiting season. It is the hardest, yet the most crucial, aspect of the walk with God. It is the time where our faith is put to test, where our hope is examined, and our trust is appraised.

"Do you really trust me?" "Do you really have faith?"

"Am I really all that you hope in?"

The silent seasons of our lives are the times where we are at war in the spiritual realm. Even with faith built so strong, the devil tries to destroy our belief. It is in these seasons that we become overwhelmed, frustrated, hurt, disappointed, and confused. We question God. We pray. We fast. We ask for godly counsel. We hope. We become afraid and we shut down.

The thing is that we experience more episodes like this, as we grow stronger in God. But my question to you today is, "Are your reactions the same?"

As we grow spiritually, we must also grow in our physical responses to situations that we have no control over. Instead of allowing ourselves to wallow in pain, confusion, hurt and disappointment, we must CHANGE THE GAME! The devil knows that if he can simply occupy our minds during these seasons, we will fail, but if we change the game, he will fail.

When you reach the next waiting season, I want you to embrace it with God and load up on the Word like never before. Remember that after every storm the sun shines, and after every test is a testimony. Rebuke fear and replace it with faith! When the devil tries to whisper sweet nothings into your ears, turn up that worship music and sing songs of praise. When the principalities remind you of how you've failed, bombard them with all your successes! Never give up! Fight and win the battle!

Tell yourself today - I'm changing the game!

Action Point – Declaration:

Make this declaration Today, I am changing the game! I am confident that no weapon formed against me will prosper and every tongue that rises against me in judgment is condemned. I am putting my smile back on my face, turning my worship music even louder, and I am equipping myself with the tools necessary for battle.[48] I am ready. I am changing the game!

---

[48] Ephesians 6:13-18

19. Silence

"If the skies are shut up and there is no rain because your people have sinned against you, and if they pray toward this Temple and acknowledge your name and turn from their sins because you have punished them, then hear from heaven and forgive the sins of your servants, your people Israel. Teach them to follow the right path, and send rain on your land that you have given to your people as their special possession."

1 Kings 8:35-36 NLT

I remember a period in my life when I felt like God was angry with me. That was the only answer that I could give then because nothing was going right. It felt like the world was against me. Everything I did failed. In my mind at that time, it would only make sense that God was mad at me because I wasn't right! I wasn't right with God, I wasn't right with myself.

I prayed and got no answer! I planned on doing things right and they ended up wrong. I smiled and received frowns. The hatred I received pierced my heart and then there was no answer from God. Now, that was the worst. I got so low that I was scared to pray. I was scared of Him rejecting my prayers again, which was what I thought had been happening. Everyday Satan reminded me of how worthless I was. He reminded me of my failures and how everyone already told me that I would be nothing. I always said to myself, "Why should God listen to you anyway, when there are so many people serving Him the right way?"

I beat myself up for months; I refused to pray and just continued my daily routine as one that wasn't expectant. Then God sent a message to me through a man in a train station who wasn't dressed the part. He didn't have on a suit and wasn't holding a microphone. He wasn't in the church and he didn't have an entourage. He was wearing dirty clothes and had a sign saying *Homeless but Hopeful*. As I was walking, I looked to my right and saw him and he said to me, "I know you're hurting but God said He loves you", I felt my heart skip a beat. I got on the train and the tears began to flow. Thoughts began to run through my mind - so there is no perfect picture, there is no perfect Christian, and He still loves me despite my flaws? I ran home and went into my room, locked the door behind me, fell on my knees and began to ask God for forgiveness. I told him I had felt like He wasn't listening. I told Him I knew I failed Him. I told Him that I went astray and was scared to speak to Him. After I poured out my heart, I sat in silence and listened; I waited for His response. God told me that He was right beside me. "I have never left your presence My child". These were the words that I heard and right after that, I felt an unimaginable peace! A heavy weight was lifted off of me.

I don't know what you're going through at this point in your life, but I want to tell you I know you're hurting but God loves you. He loves you just as you are; He loves you even though you are full of sin. He loves you even though you rejected him. He loves you even if you have failed him. He loves you even if you chose not to love him in the past.

He loves you and wants your heart; accept Him today.

Action Point - Prayer:

Dear Jesus, I am so grateful for your love. Please forgive me Lord for doubting you. Help me to embrace the inner peace that comes from a relationship with you. Help me to be patient and wait for your instructions. In Jesus name I pray. Amen.

20. Wisdom from Above

In every matter of wisdom and understanding about which the king questioned them, he found them ten times better than all the magicians and enchanters in his whole kingdom.

Daniel 1:20 NIV

There is nothing God desires more than to see you succeed and achieve all that He has planned for you. The principalities in high places know and understand this and that is why they constantly bring obstacles to try and make you fall. But regardless of what Satan might put before you, God will always turn it around for your good, it will work in your favour.

You intended to harm me, but God intended it for good to accomplish what is now being done, the saving of many lives.[49]

Daniel can attest to this. When he was taken into captivity in Babylon, he wasn't sure of what would become of him but he trusted in God. I'm sure he was physically afraid but he didn't allow his fear to overcome his faith. He knew he had to stay focused and he did exactly that. The Bible records that *"Whenever the king consulted them in any matter requiring wisdom and balanced judgment, he found them (Daniel and his three friends) to be TEN TIMES wiser than his mates."*

The power in this scripture is beyond words. Daniel was put in an unexpected situation yet he trusted in God. He did not look for a way out other than seeking the help of God. He was not distracted by the noise the other noble men or royal family members made or the talents they had.

We ought to do the same.

When I was in college, I had an instructor who constantly gave me a hard time; I could never do right by this person. It was so frustrating that at times I felt like giving up, I felt like a failure, until the day I came across Daniel 1:20. Now, I had read this verse in Daniel before but it spoke to me differently that day, all I could think of was he was TEN TIMES wiser than his mates! TEN TIMES! I began to claim the same anointing for my life as I prayed.

I had a major exam the following week. Every student that had previously taken the class already informed my friends and I of how this exam was the worst of all. I decided that it was time to step into the shoes of Daniel and trust God to hear my cry. So, that week as I fasted and prayed, I refrained from everything I could think of that would defile me. On the day of the exam, fear tried to possess my heart but I snatched it back. I took the exam and I can humbly declare to you that I received

---

[49] Genesis 50:20

the highest grade on that exam - I only missed one question; even the instructor was surprised by the result.

What's my point? God is still working the miracles of the days of Daniel. He can give you wisdom that surpasses human imagination. That day I stood ten times wiser than my mates! Glory to God.

Action Point - Prayers:

If you are seeking wisdom in any aspect of your life, use the scriptures listed below and today's text to follow the pattern that Daniel followed. Remove anything that will defile you from God, fast and pray, work on an intimate relationship with God and – WATCH GOD WORK.

Pray through the following scriptures:

- Psalm 119:126

- Psalm 119:99

Forward

~ Debbie ~

1. What's Love Got To Do With It?

So we have come to know and to believe the love that God has for us.
God is love, and whoever abides in love abides in God, and God abides in him.

1 John 4:16 ESV

The Bible tells us that God is love. We know that He is the author of love, and for the sake of love He sent His son to die that we might be set free.

I'm always mesmerised by the love of God and often share this exciting revelation as seen in the Word, that *God is love*, but my excitement can often turn into frustration when I consider how scarce love actually is.

Love is given to us freely, yet it is scarce. Why?

Recently, I had the opportunity to work with a group of people but soon realised that once the common denominator was removed (i.e. the project that brought us all together) we soon disaggregated and found ourselves back to our separate walks in life. For the time that we were on the project, we had felt like we loved one another, but it soon became apparent that that love was limited, conditional, and in fact, wasn't love at all, even though we were working on a Christian project.

The true definition of love can be found in God because love, just like God, love cannot be described in all its uniqueness and totality. We can try, and of course we should express our love with words, but we can never really express its full meaning. Many people confuse lust with love. To lust after something is to seek after its temporary pleasure, but love trumps lust, though a thin line exists between the two, they are actually miles apart.

Love remains, but with time, lust, which is often camouflaged as love is uncovered for what it truly is.

You would have heard the saying that love is blind, but the truth is that love isn't blind, it's just that love chooses to see the beauty in everyone and in everything; love looks beyond failure and doesn't give up.

Love gives and always puts others first and above all. Love understands that God is love, the very source of love, and therefore, there is no love without God. Love is expressive and always seeks the good of others. Love is comforting and refreshing.

What's love got to do with it? Everything!

To truly appreciate the depths of love, we must be open and totally surrender our hearts to God. We must choose love over lust every time. Only then will God fill our lives to the point that it overflows with love.

May the love of God, the love that is God, fill us and flow through us to touch and impact the lives of others.

Action Point – Let Us Pray:

Father we pray for Your love today. Let Your love fill our hearts to overflowing. Teach us how to love one another in a way that pleases You. Help us to discern the difference between lust and love and help us to choose love over lust every single time. And Lord, even when it seems that our love is being taken for granted, help us to stay true and help us to keep on loving, regardless. Help us to remember that love, love that comes from You, has everything to do with it.

2. It's All About You Jesus!

I am the Lord, that is My name; and My glory
I will not give to another, nor My praise to carved images.

Isaiah 42:8 NKJV

Whatever platform life gives you to spring forth, whatever stage your skills elevate you to, always point the finger of praise and glory to the One who sits above, the One who owns the throne in heaven and unquestionably and unapologetically does as He pleases. When you choose to take God's glory for yourself, then you have set yourself up as an idol, a deity, a god; by doing so, you engage the fury of Jehovah, and with idols, God will never share His glory.[50]

Many times we find ourselves in promoted positions, high up the ladder of affluence, influence, authority, and power, and then forget that we are merely dust,[51] having achieved that elevated status by grace; HIS grace. When we forget God and make it all about ourselves, that's when pride sets in and as we have come to find in scripture (as was the case with Lucifer),[52] pride destroys lives – both physically and spiritually; God moves against those who are prideful.[53]

His word says that in all our ways we should acknowledge Him and He will in turn direct our path.[54] God is not acknowledged when we make it all about ourselves and brag about the things that HE has given us the power to do or to acquire as if it was by our own strength. However, when we acknowledge Him, when we put Him first and give Him the glory, then God is glorified, and in His sovereignty and majesty, He is able to choose to decorate our lives with His glory.[55]

It's never about you or me; it should always be about Him. The whole earth is full of His glory;[56] even the heavens declare the glory of God.[57] So, be careful to give Him the glory always, not just in your closet, but publicly too. And don't go around bragging about the supposedly *righteous* things you've done and the activities you've engaged in that were once impossible but made possible by God. When you continually humble yourself in honour and worship Him (God), and His glorious majesty; only then will you be lifted up and experience His glory.

---

[50] Isaiah 42:8
[51] Psalm 103:14
[52] Isaiah 14:12-17
[53] Proverbs 16:5
[54] Proverbs 3:6
[55] Isaiah 60:2(b)
[56] Isaiah 6:3
[57] Psalm 19:1

Action Point – Let Us Pray:

Father Lord, thank You for life. Thank You for Your grace and Your mercies, which are new every morning. Thank You because You have established me and lifted me up. All that I am is because of You and for that, I return all the glory to You. Help me to always remember that You deserve all of the glory and that I can only partake of Your glory as You permit. Decorate my life with the kind of glory that the world will see and praise You and You alone. Shine through me and in me in Jesus name. Amen.

3. Ceaseless Prayer

Pray without ceasing.

1 Thessalonians 5:17 NKJV

I remember when I was younger, as a child in our house, we had periods of the day when we'd gather as a family and pray. Typically every 3 hours, and this started from as early as 6am with our only saving grace being during school hours when my siblings and I were away from home. My mum even had a bell we'd ring to signify that it was prayer time. It was a family tradition, (well at least that's what I thought and we still do it today when we gather), but also a routine and in the course of time, its value went unappreciated by the young Debbie. Back then, although we were forced to pray; it introduced some orderliness, structure, and foundation into my prayer lifestyle, which I later came to appreciate.

Typically, prayer was confined to either prayer times when we gathered as a family; or during prayer sessions in church on Sundays. I didn't appreciate personal prayer time at all and neither did I understand the need for it. Prayer was more of a religious act, rather than a form of communication with 'God' (as I heard many people claim), and besides all that, I had assumed God wouldn't listen to me anyway.

Fast forward a few decades (not that it had to take that long, but I was stubborn) and with time, spiritual growth, and maturity, I've come to learn that prayer is not just a string of intellectual words eloquently strung together and offered at a set time of the day, rather it is an intentional and intimate expression of our heart to God where He listens and then responds; much like a child and her dad having a chat during an intimate time together. It took me a long time to get to the place where God talked back (He always did, I just wasn't aware or perhaps I was not listening) but as I learnt more about prayer, I realised that He did indeed speak.

Prayer is not confined to a place, time, or location. It's not set apart for the elite or a specific denomination. Prayer is an intimate engagement that we are all privy to and an activity that should continue beyond specific moments in the day. It is a time to bare it all before God, to be completely transparent and naked before Him, like Adam and Eve before the fall; it is a time to surrender everything and expose our vulnerabilities and total dependency on God. It's a time to surrender again and again all that we are and all that we have, and then listen to His wise counsel.

Wherever you are and whatever time it is, cease every opportunity to speak to God. Unlike mankind, including family and loved ones, He is there right by your side, He will never leave you nor forsake you. I am continually mesmerised by the sheer fact, that God is always ready to listen and always ready to converse. He listens and He can hear what others can't - the beat of your heart, the sound of your tears, the whispers of your thoughts, and the expressions of your soul.

Corporate prayer is good, but it is only in the secret place, in private, that we can share our innermost thoughts, feelings, emotions, and expressions with God - exposed, unashamed, uninhibited, and in the most transparent and candid way. It is in the secret place that we can lay it all bare and submit everything to God.

Action Point - Meditation:

- Consider; how can you engage in communion (conversation) throughout your day with God?

- Remember, it is the desire of God's heart that we commune with Him always, every moment of every day. So, dear friends, pray without ceasing, and cease every opportunity to pray! Deliberately take some time to speak to God today and do all you can to continue that conversation throughout the day.

4. Jesus, Where Are You?

But supposing Him to have been in the company, they went a day's journey, and sought Him among their relatives and acquaintances. So when they did not find Him, they returned to Jerusalem, seeking Him. Now so it was that after three days they found Him in the temple, sitting in the midst of the teachers, both listening to them and asking them questions.

Luke 2:44-46 NKJV

Have you ever gotten so relaxed and been so trusting of a loved one that you just assumed they'd always be there? I often have. For example, there have been times when I've been exposed to a new venture and I've already counted on the support of a friend or family member in my mind during my planning stages, only to later find that they are not as passionate as I had thought they would be and so, their support was lacking.

There have been seasons when I've been challenged by tough times and before I could turn around and lean on someone I trusted for support, those that I expected to *have my back* were the very ones stabbing me in the back, or were just nowhere to be found. I'm sure you are also able to share similar experiences.

There are periods in life when it can feel like Jesus is not there, nowhere to be found, like He has abandoned us for something or someone better, especially in the tough times; but unlike our friends and family, Jesus is the friend that is always there, He is the friend that sticks closer than a brother.[58]

In our text today, we read that after a while, Jesus' parents realised that Jesus was no longer in their midst. Many times in our lives too, if we are not careful, we may come to find that Jesus is no longer in our midst, no longer at the centre of where we are, or no longer engaged in what we are doing. It may seem like Jesus has *moved on,* but when you take a closer look, you'll find out that you are actually the one that has moved away or walked out on Him. This is usually as a result of habitual sin, or a misdirected focus when experiencing rough times.

When we feel like asking Jesus *"Where are You?"* this is an indication that we need to refocus our minds on Him and seek Him where He can be found. When Jesus' earthly parents found Him, He was in the temple, engaging the word. Jesus is the Word, the Living Word, and that is one place where He can always be found. In the word. Whether we are going through the highs or lows of life, instead of asking Jesus, where He is, or allowing our situation(s) to lead us away from Him, we should expose our minds and our situation(s) to the Word of God. The key to sticking with Jesus is to ensure that you plant your feet right where He wants you to be, right by

---

[58] Proverbs 18:24

His side, right where He has placed or is placing you, and the best way of understanding that is by becoming intimate with His word.[59]

Seasons of weariness and loneliness are likely to come as we navigate through life; it may even feel as if God has abandoned us or Jesus is nowhere to be found. Jesus is never lost! Let me say that again, Jesus is NEVER lost but sometimes we get lost and then expect to find Jesus after we have drifted away. Seek Him where (while) He can be found,[60] look for Him in His word, and work on developing a deeper relationship with Him. Oftentimes, I have seasons of drought when I feel spiritually weak and I have come to discover that this happens when I spend less time in God's presence or when I have strayed.

Dear friend, don't let your feelings and emotions be the navigation that guides you, but instead rely and depend upon the Spirit of God, who bears witness with our spirit[61] and leads us.[62] When your spirit craves a refreshing, a revival or a rejuvenation, be intentional about creating (more) time to spend with God and to nurture your spirit: pick up the Bible, read, study, and meditate. Surround yourself with other Christian brothers and sisters, and find pockets of time to have a retreat, a one on one with God.

Remember that God is love, foster love, encourage love, and seek depth in the expression of the love of Christ in everything. Jesus was found not just where the Word was being shared but in the midst of love and fellowship, a place of refreshing, renewal, and transformation.

Action Point - Let Us Pray:

Father today I pray that I will always be sensitive to Your leading, and faithful enough to follow. Help me not to stray away from you but to remain steadfast in You, to grow in You, and in Your love. Give me a renewed and deep desire for Your love and Your Word. Reveal Yourself to me in a fresh way and help me to always stay where your grace is.

Whenever I feel like asking, *"where are You Lord"*, help me to see that You are still with me and never left, help me to identify where I may have drifted away from You. Help me find the way, lead me back to You. In Jesus name. Amen.

---

[59] Psalm 119:105
[60] Isaiah 55:6-7, Proverb 8:17
[61] Romans 8:16
[62] Galatians 5:25

5. Hiding the Word

Your word I have hidden in my heart,
that I might not sin against You.

Psalm 119:11 NKJV

To hide the word of God in your heart means to read, study, meditate, reflect upon, and imbibe that word; and then to store it in your heart, by committing it to memory. When you hide God's word in your heart, you have a constant reminder, the word of God, germinating in your heart for the right time and for all time – guarding and guiding your heart. Once in your heart, the word of God will convict you of sin, it will transform you and when the devil tries to invade your heart (mind), what does he find there? He finds the Word of God, Jesus. Therefore, the heart is an incredibly unique and smart place to keep the word of God.

It's great for those of us living in the Western World who are able to carry our Bibles around freely, or have them loaded on our mobile devices, but there are other parts of the world where this is forbidden and illegal!

The word of God is powerful, sharper than any two-edged sword,[63] the enemy knows that there is power in the word of God. I mean, Jesus exalts His word above His name,[64] and so, the enemy goes to work trying to pervert, twist, and distort the word of God by instilling confusing words, ideologies and false doctrines into our hearts to challenge the word of God. If you have nothing in your heart, or you have not worked on increasing the word of God in your heart, then the devil is in for a field day with your heart and emotions – remember he goes around roaring like a lion seeking whom to devour.[65] This is why at certain times, we may hear confusing voices in our head, whilst many more are falling prey, mistaking the voice of the enemy for the voice of God.

Jesus said, *"My sheep hear my voice"*[66] and the best way to learn to hear and follow the voice of the Lord, is by storing His words in our hearts, replaying it at every opportunity (perhaps by reciting memory verses or even singing scripture), so that when we need them, they are readily available, printed in our memories, speaking life to our very souls, motivating and encouraging us to act on that word. Hiding the word of God in our hearts helps us by the power of the Holy Spirit to be able to discern the voice of the enemy. When we know God, when we know His word and become accustomed to His voice, we will not be exploited by the whispers of the enemy or the noise of the world. Remember that it is those that KNOW their God

---

[63] Hebrews 4:12
[64] Psalm 138:2
[65] 1 Peter 5:8
[66] John 10:27

that shall be strong and do exploits;[67] it goes to show that those who do not know their God will be weak and be exploited, right? Knowing God is equivalent to knowing His word, living His word, and I dare to say becoming 'the word' (well, allowing it to shape and form you) by allowing that WORD to live in us and act out its purpose and will through us.

Reading the word is good, but we must graduate to studying and meditating on the Bible. Personally, I have come to find that the more I meditate on the words I've read, ask questions, read commentaries, and write my own thoughts (as led by the Spirit of God), the more I am able to imbibe the word; literally EAT IT!!!!

"Your words were found, and I ate them, And Your word was to me the joy and rejoicing of my heart; For I am called by Your name, O LORD God of hosts."

Jeremiah 15:16 NKJV

Action Point - Reflection:

Make a resolve today to go to the buffet table (breakfast, lunch, and dinner) where you can eat and never get full. You might need to take time to digest and ruminate, but you will find that the more you eat at the table, the sweeter it gets and the more you want. At the table your plate is always full, and your cup runs over with all the right spiritual ingredients and nutrients. At the table, there is no dieting or fasting (only fools even think about doing such).

The table is set, the food is ready; will you eat?

---

[67] Daniel 11:32b

6. Heavenly Wealth

*"Don't wear yourself out trying to get rich. Be wise enough to know when to quit.
In the blink of an eye wealth disappears, for it will sprout wings and fly away like
an eagle."*

Proverbs 23:4-5 NLT

With wisdom comes understanding and the more you meditate on the word of God, the more you will come to realise that true wealth comes from God. Such wealth lasts forever, yes, even for eternity. It doesn't grow wings and fly away; it doesn't fizzle out and rust. It doesn't get devalued or degraded. Eternal wealth gives everlasting peace and joy, layered with long life and good health.

Often enough, people work so hard in order to put way too much food on the table to build a career and an empire that no one really cares about but you - it certainly is not to God's glory. When they eventually get a minute to look up, all the money is spent and so, the vicious cycle starts again.

In some cases, they accumulate so much wealth and then have no time left to enjoy it. I once knew of a lady who was hard working. She had about three jobs outside of the home and literally worked every hour she could. She eventually wore herself out working so hard that she died – on the job! After her death, it came to light that she had close to a million in the bank and didn't need to work so hard. A single woman, almost 60 died because she was busy trying to accumulate so much wealth that she would never live to enjoy.

She, like many others, missed out on life because she was too busy accumulating riches to notice the birds sing, the flowers blossom, or even the children around her grow up. Unfortunately, many people like this exist that just haven't read their Bibles enough, or developed spiritual maturity to realise that true wealth comes from spending time with God and obeying His word.

Still, others look for get rich quick schemes and before long, they've exhausted all their savings, trying to get rich, and end up worse off than when they started. Statistics show that 70% of those who play the lottery actually end up bankrupt. This buttresses the fact that those who are looking for quick riches will get into trouble.[68]

I heard of a man who spent his years working hard, using all his savings to build houses for his four children in Africa. The tragedy was that those children lived abroad all their lives, and after his death didn't even return to Africa to claim the houses their father had built for them. They were not interested, and some of the houses were taken over by unknown family members; I learnt that one of the houses remained empty and soon became derelict. What a waste!

---

[68] Proverbs 28:20

I pray that God will teach us to seek after Him, the greatest treasure of our life. The One who owns the cattle upon a thousand hills[69] and holds the whole world in His hands.[70] Amen.

I leave you with this scripture:

> *Don't store up treasures here on earth, where moths eat them and rust destroys them, and where thieves break in and steal. Store your treasures in heaven, where moths and rust cannot destroy, and thieves do not break in and steal. Wherever your treasure is, there the desires of your heart will also be.*

Matt 6:19-21 NLT

Action Point - Meditation:

Meditate on the scripture given above. Consider all the ways that you may have been travailing after worldly riches instead of heavenly wealth. Now pray and make a decision to let go of the desire and lust for worldly things. Finally, write down five things that you will start to do to seek after heavenly treasures.

_____
_____
_____
_____
_____
_____
_____
_____
_____
_____
_____
_____
_____
_____
_____
_____
_____
_____

[69] Psalm 50:10-12
[70] Psalm 95:4

7. Loving Others

"Don't be selfish; don't try to impress others. Be humble, thinking of others as better than yourselves. Don't look out only for your own interests, but take an interest in others, too."

Philippians 2:3-4 NLT

The greatest law is highlighted in Matt 22:37-40, and most people know what it says even without referencing the Bible passage. It is to *"love the Lord your God with all your heart, all your soul, and all your mind; and the second which is equally important, is to love your neighbour as yourself".*

What I love about today's scripture is that it gives us practical ways in which we can love our neighbour.

Let's break it down:

1. **Don't be selfish.** We live in a world that has taught us that we only live once, so we should maximise it, simply put - anything goes. Yes, we have one life to live here on earth but we owe it to God and to ourselves to live that life in the right way. The greatest commandment is the commandment of love, to love God and to love others; it is not to love yourself.[71] A selfish person cannot truly love someone else, because they will ultimately put themselves first. Loving others as we love ourselves means that what we value as good for ourselves is what we should offer unto others. We shouldn't treat people in the way that we would not want to be treated.[72] Let's not be selfish and start being loving, loving of God and of others. As God has extended His arm of love to us, we should also extend an arm of love to others.

2. **Don't try to impress others.** We live in the world of *"I"*, where *"I"* is king, the time and seasons where the 'selfie', and live videos (Snapchat, Instagram and the like) are the rage and your social media clout measurement is uppermost on your mind. I have been to wedding parties and other occasions only to see people dancing with their phones as they 'live stream' themselves dancing. You turn on the news and hear of youngsters depressed even to the point of suicide because they were unable to impress people and achieve high numbers of virtual attention to their selfies that they post online. We should live to impress God by following His standards as laid out in the word. Worldly applause and accolades are but for a moment, but everlasting joy and the reward that comes from obedience to the *WORD* of God is eternal. Live to impress God and not people.[73]

---

[71] Matthew 22:37-38
[72] Luke 6:31
[73] Colossians 3:23

3. **Be humble.** Arrogance and pride kill.[74] It can kill everything that God has placed in you and make you miss the mark. The reward for remaining humble is far greater than that, and not worth the price of pride and arrogance, ask Lucifer. Humility is not stupidity but wisdom! When you humble yourself, God Himself will lift you up. Remember, God resists the proud but gives grace to the humble.[75]

4. **Thinking of others better than yourself.** Now that's a hard one in this narcissist world when nearly everything we do is for the betterment of self. The godly way however is to think of others better than yourself. When we do this, it helps us to keep ourselves in check. Then we will not be selfish or strive to impress others. A good way to do this is to see others through the lens of the Word and the eyes of God. There is a gem, a treasure in everybody, so seek out the good in others; you'll find that by doing so you are empowering them to greatness and loving them as you have been commanded to do.

5. **Don't look out only for your own interest but take an interest in others too.** Yep! The things that interest you are great and can help you to discover your purpose and the things that God has placed in you, however, if you concentrate on the things that interest you alone, you are at risk of becoming selfish and self-centred. Remember the second greatest commandment. Take interest in others and help them stir up the gifts of God in them, you are to be your brother's keeper!

Finally, live for Christ in accordance with His word, and let the world see and be attracted to the Christ in you.[76] Christ is not selfish, He is not arrogant, and certainly didn't live to impress Himself. He thought of others more highly than Himself such that it pushed Him to the cross. And even though He was of *"equal status"* with God, He humbled Himself to become like man - for you and I.[77]

Action Point – Memory Challenge:

- Pray through today's scripture as you pray for yourself

- Commit the scripture (Phil 2:3-4) to memory and recite it every day for the next 7 days

- Write it out in the space below if that helps

---

[74] Proverbs 16:18
[75] James 4:6, 10
[76] Galatians 2:20
[77] Philippians 2:6-7

8. Are You A Thornbush?

I love this parable:

"Once upon a time the trees decided to choose a king. First, they said to the olive tree, 'Be our king!' But the olive tree refused, saying, 'Should I quit producing the olive oil that blesses both God and people, just to wave back and forth over the trees?' "Then they said to the fig tree, 'You be our king!' But the fig tree also refused, saying, 'Should I quit producing my sweet fruit just to wave back and forth over the trees?' "Then they said to the grapevine, 'You be our king!' But the grapevine also refused, saying, 'Should I quit producing the wine that cheers both God and people, just to wave back and forth over the trees?' "Then all the trees finally turned to the thornbush and said, 'Come, you be our king!' And the thornbush replied to the trees, 'If you truly want to make me your king, come and take shelter in my shade. If not, let fire come out from me and devour the cedars of Lebanon.'"

Judges 9:8-15 NLT

In my youth, while in secondary school, I had a period when I was just a little bit of a troublemaker. To be completely honest, and with the benefit of hindsight, I think it's because I was unfulfilled with life, had a low self-esteem, and was seeking attention. Growing up in a poor community with a single parent and plagued with numerous health challenges was not an ideal place to be - neither an excuse - but unbeknownst to me, I let it get the better of me and consequently did a lot of foolish things.

My mum was a regular visitor to the school office singing about our religious practices and our love for God which frustrated me greatly, but I was pumped by the accolades and attention from my 'friends' as I was encouraged by their incitement and played to the things that pleased them; like standing on the table in class and disrespectfully talking back to the teacher. At all cost I was to be their 'leader,' you know the tough girl that everyone listened to/respected. The irony is that I was the one listening to their commands.

As a mature adult, and thank God for maturity in Christ, I have learned the errors of my ways. I am grateful that it was a temporary disposition (perhaps a phase) that I was able to escape, but it is one that plagues many adults, even in Christendom today. Many have installed themselves as 'leaders' and 'kings' over others outside the authority of God, which can and will inevitably lead to dire consequences.

The above extract shared from the book of Judges references a time after Gideon's death that his son Abimelech became a rogue and killed his 70 siblings just to become king over the people. His brother, Jotham was the only one who managed to escape his craziness. In search for authority and power, Abimelech allowed evil to consume his heart and became like the thornbush inviting the people to take shade under his cover and authority. A quick study of thornbushes or bramble (NKJV) reveals that it can be poisonous, killing all fruit bearing vegetation that grows near it.

Are you a thornbush seeking or chasing authority where God has not sent you and where you clearly do not fit in? Have you been given power in a place of authority but you know that your motives are questionable or not right? Perhaps you have been responsible for installing someone into a position that God has not called them to. It is time to take stock, to repent, and to make amends. Everything and everyone that God made is *'fit for purpose'*, and therefore, we should remain where God has placed us, blossom there and make God proud.

Action Point - Let Us Pray:

Father, I am sorry for all the times that I have chased after power and authority in places where You have not called me, rather than submit to Your power and authority, and remain where You have placed me. Father, help me to appreciate my sphere of influence and to execute it righteously. I pray that I will not seek after the promotion that comes from man but rather the elevation that comes from You. In Jesus name. Amen.

9. Who Do You Look Like?

Then God said, "Let us make human beings in our image, to be like us. They will reign over the fish in the sea, the birds in the sky, the livestock, all the wild animals on the earth, and the small animals that scurry along the ground."

Genesis 1:26 NLT

Some look like their mums, others look like their dads and that's all good, but regardless of whom you look like, you'll have the characteristics and DNA of both.

With God, we only have one parent, the Father. We were made in His image and so, it follows that we will (well, should) look like Him, but our reflection of His image became distorted when sin came knocking and we (in the loins of Adam and Eve) opened the door! At that point, the Bible does not record that there were any physical changes to our persona, so we can conclude that perhaps there were none, but make no mistake, our spiritual resemblance changed. God is a spirit and so are we; our spiritual appearance was distorted so that we no longer looked like God.

The Bible makes it clear that the eyes of the Lord are too pure to behold evil[78] and so the Spirit of God withdraws when we conform to wickedness and make it a lifestyle. The two cannot coincide. Either darkness makes way for light, or we switch the light off and permit darkness to flow! How sad since we are called light.[79]

Jesus died to restore us to our rightful place in God, back to the image in which we were initially made. That image is in His (spiritual) looks, His characteristics, His heart, but restoration and redemption are not automatic – rather:

- They are to as many who receive and believe in Him[80].

- They are to those who will receive salvation and guard it with fear and trembling.[81];

- They are to those who pursue the mind of Christ[82] daily by renewing and transforming their mind through the word of God.[83]

- They are to those who think on heavenly things.[84]

---

[78] Habakkuk 1:13
[79] Matthew 5:14-16
[80] John 1:12
[81] Philippians 2:12
[82] 1 Corinthians 2:16
[83] Romans 12:2
[84] Colossians 3:2

- They are to those who walk in the Spirit and pursue the fruit of the Spirit.[85]

- They are to those who know that the heart of man is desperately wicked[86] and so allow God to do a heart transplant, exchanging their heart of stone for a heart of flesh.[87]

When you get this right, you will look in the mirror and notice a difference even though the transformation is inward (inside out). Others will look at you and testify that your character, who you really are, is like a breath of fresh air, is life giving even to dry bones because you are the child of your Father and you *look* like him.

Have you ever heard how spouses begin to look like each other as the years of their relationship and intimacy roll on? Actually, there are no physical changes; it is an inward likeness that is reflected on the outside. The same is true with God. The more time you spend in His presence, praying, worship, studying to be more like Him, the more you will attain it. Enoch is an example of one who became so much 'like' God that he disappeared inside God.

It's not impossible to be *like* God, and to look like God, because if it were (impossible), God would not have made us in His image and *God doesn't make mistakes.* He has given us the Holy Spirit that works in us a good work and helps to transform our character until we display the fruit of the Spirit rather than the works of the flesh.

Action Point - Activity:

Resolve to do everything you can to get rid of those things that stop you from looking like God and start reflecting the image of the Most High God. If it helps, write down all the things that you need to stop doing, and make a list of all the great things that you can start doing right away to make God proud. Use the fruit of the spirit as listed in Galatians 5:22-23 as a guide to build your character and your 'looks' to be more like God.

---

[85] Galatians 5:16-25
[86] Jeremiah 17:9
[87] Ezekiel 36:26

Things I need to STOP doing:

_____

_____

_____

_____

_____

_____

_____

_____

_____

_____

_____

_____

_____

Things I need to START doing:

_____

_____

_____

_____

_____

_____

_____

_____

_____

_____

_____

_____

_____

10. The Cup

*And David said with longing, "Oh, that someone would give me a drink of the
water from the well of Bethlehem, which is by the gate!" So the three mighty
men broke through the camp of the Philistines, drew water from the well of
Bethlehem that was by the gate, and took it and brought it to David.
Nevertheless he would not drink it, but poured it out to the Lord. And he said,
"Far be it from me, Lord, that I should do this! Is this not the blood of the men
who went in jeopardy of their lives?" Therefore he would not drink it. These
things were done by
the three mighty men.*

2 Samuel 23:15-17 NKJV

Grabbing the disposal cup of hot water I had prepared that morning to soothe my
sore throat, I ran swiftly but carefully out of my house. Only seven minutes left to
catch my morning train to work and walking just wouldn't cut it. As I ran, I
considered the 'poshness' of my steps and was translated back in time.

Suddenly, I was one of the three mighty men in the time of David and I found myself
holding onto the cup of water to quench David's thirst as I simultaneously dodged
and negotiated the arrows of the enemy. It was tough, it was hard work; the only
water that dropped to the ground was the sweat of my brow but it had to be done
because the master required it.

What a service!

Then the Lord reminded me of the cup in Psalm 23:5, the one that overflows with
oil in the midst of my enemies.

What a contrast!

On the one hand I managed to balance, sustain and keep the cup full for the master
despite the destructive and distractive nature of the war which raged, yet on the other
hand the water, now oil was overflowing in this cup. In this vision/translation back
in time, I had been anointed especially for my service (to carry the cup) despite the
hard times, and both events were in full sight and on show for my enemies to see.
Hallelujah!

As I stumbled onto the train, I started to consider the message and the lessons that
my Father was teaching me which I share with you now:

1. The mighty men in today's scripture were not distracted, despite the raging war,
    the situation they faced, or the circumstances that surrounded them.

2. The men remained focused, their gaze fixed on the goal: to get water and return
    safely. They had the master on their mind and risked their lives - in effect

becoming a living sacrifice for the master. Like the three Hebrew men in the furnace of fire,[88] or like Esther,[89] they were ready to die to accomplish the mission in their service to their master.

3. The men got the water from the exact well as requested, by the gate of Bethlehem. It's possible that there were other wells along the way (even in Bethlehem) but they didn't look for a counterfeit or a fake. They were obedient without compromise (even though David had not made a direct request of them).

4. They gave the master what he longed for, what he required. They must have had a very good personal relationship with David to understand and value his desires.

5. It was considered quality sacrifice and even worship, so much that David considered it as the life and blood of the mighty men and offered it to the One who was worthy of such a quality sacrifice.

Action Point – Meditation:

Here are some questions to consider for meditation:

- What are your goals in life? Where are you going?

- Are you distracted by the ploys and plot of the enemy?

- How are you navigating life? Do you know exactly where you are going?

- Is your destination aligned to the Master's will?

- Do you know what He desires of you?

- What is your relationship with the Father like? Is it intimate?

- What is the sacrifice you bring to the Lord? Is that sacrifice of great quality?

- Are you the sacrifice that you bring?

- Are you a living sacrifice?

Final thoughts: The cup can be considered as your life, which you hold on to as you carefully run the race of life. Jesus is longing for that cup which He wants to offer to God. Ensure you are running the right race, your race. Don't let the distractions of

---

[88] Daniel 3:23
[89] Esther 4:16

73

life or the enemy stop you from reaching the finish line or steal the contents of your cup by emptying it completely along the way. Instead, hand your cup over to Jesus, He will keep it safe and secure and ensure that it overflows with His Spirit.

Use the space below to take some note during your meditation period:

----

11. Procrastination Playground

I say then: Walk in the Spirit, and you shall not fulfill the lust of the flesh.
For the flesh lusts against the Spirit, and the Spirit against the flesh; and these are
contrary to one another, so that you do not do the things that you wish.

Galatians 5:16-17 NKJV

Have you ever had a deep desire to do something but despite that passion, and against all odds, you found yourself playing around in Procrastination Playground? I've been in that playground before, well several times, dreaming on the swings and sliding gracefully on the slides. So, you can see that I'm no stranger in this very playground, and whilst the spirit is willing, the flesh is very weak, but no more excuses, I have been praying[90] and working earnestly on a strategy to get out once and for all, and so should you.

You see, many times when we visit Procrastination Playground, it is usually because whilst we want the benefits that are infused in the required action of the moment, we become lazy, fatigued, and weak, and take no action.

What about you? What are you procrastinating on?

Perhaps God has been speaking to you about a specific project, or calling you to reach out to someone else, but even though you have been hearing God, you deny it and suggest that perhaps somehow, that's not what God means. For many of us, God has been calling us into a deep, personal, and one on one fellowship with Him, nothing like before but something different, something new. He requires that we spend more time in His word, singing in adoration to Him and meditating on the revelations that He gives us.

Consider the Spirit, Soul, and Body in their most basic terms and the part each play in the never-ending procrastination cycle.

- **Spirit:** The spirit is activated in the believer when he or she accepts Jesus into his or her life and receives the gift of salvation. The spirit enables us to have an intimate relationship with God, God is a Spirit and those who worship Him must do so in spirit and in truth.[91]

- **Soul:** The soul is the part of man that allows him to connect with other people. It holds our minds, wills, emotions, and other intangible elements of our being. It is indifferent and will sway towards the most influential parts of who we are, i.e. spirit or body.

- **Body:** The body is bent on indulging in fleshly desires, materialistic things, e.g. secular elements.

---

[90] Matthew 26:41
[91] John 4:23-24

Among these three entities, a war engulfs. It's a struggle, a continuous, daily war, and one that will continue till the end of this lifetime. The question of who wins the war depends on the most influential entity of the three, and since the soul is indifferent, it will either be the spirit or the flesh. The winner will be the entity that we feed and nurture on a daily basis, and that's where many of us fail and allow procrastination to creep in. Our Lord knows we cannot overcome the flesh by ourselves and need divine intervention to start putting our flesh under submission.[92]

One sure way I have found of subjecting (weakening) the flesh is through fasting. I find it easier to fast when I speak to my flesh directly. When the hunger pangs set in, I simply look myself in the mirror and say: "Body, you do not control me, I control you and I'm telling you there's no food until the set time. Get it right!" I find that after a little while I am no longer hungry and am able to redirect my focus and attention to the word, to fasting, and to praying during that time which in turn strengthens my spirit, soul and weakens my body. The power to control my body ultimately comes from the Spirit of God speaking in me, through me, and to me.

So, I beseech thee today (in King James speech ☺), do not give in to the flesh but rather to the spirit. Spend time feeding and nurturing the spirit so that He may increase in you and you may decrease.[93] The body must not win the war, the spirit must! God has never lost a battle and so, when we allow Him to strengthen our spirits, then the battle is won and the flesh will be brought under subjection, procrastination will not win. I pray that God will help us as we seek to die to the flesh (and of course procrastination) daily and increase our spirit since the spirit is indeed willing. No more procrastination, especially of the things of the Spirit!

Goodbye Procrastination Playground!

Action Point - Activity:

Consider the areas that you have been wallowing in procrastination. Write them down on the next page. Now consider how you can make changes to rebut each procrastination point. Make a resolve to turn every procrastination point into a productivity and progress point. Be sure to revisit the next page regularly (at least monthly) to review your progress against each point you've made. Pray during the month about these areas where you clearly need divine intervention and be intentional about making changes that accelerate progress.

---

[92] 1 Corinthians 9:27
[93] John 3:30

Procrastination Points:

_____

_____

_____

_____

_____

_____

_____

_____

_____

_____

_____

_____

Progress Plan:

_____

_____

_____

_____

_____

_____

_____

_____

_____

_____

_____

_____

_____

_____

12. First Love

*"'But I have this [charge] against you, that you have left
your first love [you have lost the depth of love that you
first had for Me].'"*

Revelations 2:4 AMP

I will never forget when I first *truly* became saved, when I really appreciated God for who He was to me and who He is. I was astounded by His amazing love for me and subsequently fell deeply in love with Him. Oh, what a joy!

It's not a feeling I can adequately describe with words but it definitely comes close to when I first fell in love with my husband, or when I gave birth to my first child; but these experiences are inadequate to precisely explain that exhilaration, and that joy. This experience was renewed yet in a different and even more exciting and rewarding way when I fell in love with spending time in devotion to and with God, hearing God speak directly to me right from the pages of scriptures.

When I first fell in love with Jesus, I was very excited, I wanted the whole world to know. I sang, I shouted, I danced, I had found joy, I wanted to scream from the rooftop (it was a kind of David dancing moment[94]) but those that surrounded me were not moved by my newfound love and couldn't comprehend my expressions (a kind of Michal moment).[95]

The same is true for the second scenario - spending time in the word. In fact, many thought I was crazy; the unspoken statement their faces beheld screamed "*Is this not the same Jesus that you have always claimed to follow as a Christian?*" some even said I wasn't making sense, and that I had always been a child of God since I was a PK (Pastors' kid) born into Christianity.

It was very difficult for me to have such great love bestowed upon me by the Father, and then to love Him back, and not have anyone to share it with; not being able to take my loved ones on this exciting new journey and get them to taste, see, and experience Jesus the way that I did or create new memories in Christ together. Many of these people were friends who I grew up with, they too proclaimed Christ but like me were never really transformed into a new creature, never regenerated by the Spirit of God; they were still stuck in the bondage of sin with a disguised title of 'Christian' just like I had been before my encounter with the Lord.

I so eagerly wanted to scream and tell the whole world, like the woman at the well,[96] who after her encounter told everyone about Jesus; I wanted to scream from the rooftops and speak and sing about Him every day. Since those around me couldn't grasp what I felt, I had to find an alternative resolve, at least until I was mature enough to

---

[94] 2 Samuel 6:14
[95] 2 Samuel 6:16)
[96] John 4:28

know how to share my *love* with others without getting offended by their response(s). So, I looked for others who were already in love with Jesus and sought out gatherings where I could love Jesus unashamed, unlimited, and with the benefit of growing deeper in love with Him and more mature in my Christian walk.

Have you ever been so in love with something or someone and those around you didn't understand and maybe even laughed at you? Some men love football and would love to share this love with their wives, but the looks they get from their beloved wives at the mention of the game warns them to go no further. Whatever it is that you love, it is always so much better when you have others who are ready to share in that love; this is often my satisfaction when I attend church and other Christian gatherings with likeminded people.

After reading today's devotional, why not close your eyes and think back to that special moment when you fell in love with the Lord. That tingling sensation that you couldn't describe, that smile on your face that you couldn't get rid of. God is calling us back to that love, and to experience that feeling perpetually. See, God doesn't change, He is still the same and will always be,[97] but life distracts, life disturbs, and life distorts our joy and our focus that we forget or sometimes walk away from our love for God.

God is calling us back to the time we first fell in love with Him. Loving God and giving Him your best means falling in love with Him over and over again, every single day as if we just met Him, but with the knowledge that we can and will love Him more deeply the more we acknowledge and spend time in Him, loving Him.

God is calling you back to the love room.

Action Point - Activity:

- Spend some time meditating on your first encounter with Jesus.

- Write down the experience, how it made you feel, the emotions you felt and the joy it instilled in you.

- Do you still feel the same way?

- Where have you backslidden and turned away from God?

- What have you replaced God with, what other thing(s) are you loving instead of loving God first?

- Decide to come back to your first love, write down the changes you are going to make to come back to God.

---

[97] Hebrews 13:8

- Now say a prayer, speak to God genuinely, wholeheartedly and don't hold anything back.

Write notes for today's activity in the space provided below:

_____
_____
_____
_____
_____
_____
_____
_____
_____
_____
_____
_____
_____
_____
_____
_____
_____
_____
_____
_____
_____
_____
_____

13. The Power of Passion

For where your treasure is, there your heart will be also.

Matthew 6:21 NKJV

The Passion of the Christ was a powerful film depicting the story of a Man who was so passionate about the people He came to save. Passionate to the point of death! That passion pushed Him from heavenly glory into this world, and thereafter unto the cross. His life was offered as a sacrifice so that we may live, and live life more abundantly.

We sometimes claim that we are passionate about something or passionately in love with someone, but do we truly understand passion? Passion can be either positive or negative. Whatever the case, the power of passion will drive you miles in the direction of your passion's desire.

What are you passionate about?

Some claim passion for their lover, children, jobs, cars, gadgets, or even money.

What about God? Are you passionate about God?

Passion is powerful!

- Ask Abraham; he was so passionate about God that he was willing to sacrifice his son.[98]

- Ask Enoch; he was so passionate about God that he was <u>not</u>, i.e. he disappeared in God.[99]

- Ask Mordecai; he was so passionate about God that he refused to bow to Haman.[100].

- Ask Daniel, whose passion for God drove him into the lion's den.[101]

- Ask the three Hebrew men, whose passion drove them straight into the fiery furnace.[102]

- Ask Paul; who considered all things as dung simply that he may gain Christ[103].

---

[98] Genesis 22:10-11
[99] Genesis 5:24
[100] Esther 3:1-5
[101] Daniel 6:16
[102] Daniel 3
[103] Philippians 3:8

The results, brought about by godly passion, are immeasurable as the lives of these men of God testify. When your passion is God-inspired, you stand to benefit.[104]

Where is your passion driving you?

When a man is driven by passion, he is almost unconquerable, since passion can drive you even on water, i.e. that goal that you thought was impossible or unreachable suddenly becomes possible when passion is engaged.

Let me share a personal example with you. I've always been passionate about technology though I had never worked in the field or gained any related qualification. My passion drove me into exploring various types of software, and before long, I was on numerous self-development learning pathways. I soon acquired heaps of related magazines; signed up to numerous information websites on the subject; bought numerous books; I'd even made a few professional acquaintances right until information overload kicked in - yet my passion led me into pursuing more and eventually creating related products.

My passion for Christ, incomparable to His passion for me (might I add) stopped me dead in my tracks as I evaluated my life with and without Christ. I decided to walk step by step with Him. This resulted in a real change to the way I integrated into my local church, as I earnestly started seeking out short and intensive discipleship courses, which would later inform my faith, grow my spirit, and propel me into ministry within and outside the church. This passion also revealed a transformation in my persona and character, both spiritually and surprisingly to me, physically!

Passion accelerates you. Passion births within you an inherent attraction to keep going, and when you get to your destination, keep on going still.

Action Point - Challenge:

So, I challenge you today: what are you passionate about in comparison to what you know you should be passionate about (but are not)? How can you fuel godly passion and starve ungodly passions to death? Do a spiritual analysis today and spend more time on whatever you are doing that is godly and good, studying it and thereby empowering your passion.

Use the space below to take notes as you go through today's activity.

_____
_____
_____

[104] Matthew 6:33

14. Follow-Follow

So Elisha turned back from him, and took a yoke of oxen and slaughtered them and boiled their flesh, using the oxen's equipment, and gave it to the people, and they ate. Then he arose and followed Elijah, and became his servant.

1 Kings 19:21 NKJV

"Where is he going?" I thought to myself as I gazed at the same gyratory for the third time in twenty minutes, *"This guy is lost!"* I signalled left, pulled over, grabbed my phone and furiously entered his digits.

"Joe", I called, he didn't even notice that my car was no longer behind his. *"I'm heading back home; I know I struggle to understand that satnav but I'm going to try and find my way back home and start afresh with the satnav. Enough of these circles, it's obvious you can't remember how to get there".*

"I'm sorry love, I missed the turning that's why" he replied sheepishly, *"I remember the way now, honest. And we're nearly there."*

The merry-go-round reminded me of that saying, *'the blind leading the blind'.* I should have driven after Linda, true she'd only been to the conference in Plymouth once, but she was always on point and on track! Joe had attended this annual conference three years in a row and after two hours of driving (probably in the wrong direction), we still had no evidence of being close to our destination.

We sometimes find in life that we are driving behind the wrong car spiritually. We put our trust in someone who we believe is going where we are going, perhaps has even been there before, and told stories of his/her great journey. So, we let our guard down, forget about our own personal satnav, and follow for miles.

- Who are you following?

- Who is your mentor?

- Who are you trusting spiritually to lead you along life's journey?

- When the pitfalls come, who are you following and trusting to guide you around them, ensuring that you don't fall into the ditch that so many already have?

You may say; *"I have a Father who will never fail me"* or *"I can do all things through Christ who strengthens me"*, or even *"Jesus is my mentor"* and whilst all these are plausible to an extent, there are Biblical principles for having a spiritual mentor. Aaron had Moses, Jonathan had David, Elisha had Elijah and even Jesus Himself was a spiritual mentor to the twelve disciples.

It is necessary to have a spiritual mentor, somebody who is not necessarily elderly, but someone who is wise, who has matured in Christ, who can show and tell you some home truths that you might have become oblivious to, or can correct you when you err and are going off track; someone who is not afraid to see you succeed and will champion your growth in Christ, cheering you on from mere milk to the meat and bones.

Who is your mentor? Who are you looking up to? Who is your spiritual covering? Do you have someone who is not afraid to share his or her experiences in Christ (good and bad), someone who you are accountable to?

The storyteller (Janet) in the preceding fictional story put her trust completely in the hands of Joe, a mentor who placed his trust in his head knowledge, instincts and bearings; rather than trusting the satnav which is symbolic of the living Word of God. Had he been directed by and followed the satnav, Janet would not have been so frustrated and would have reached the final destination successfully.

A spiritual mentor is important, yet that mentor should be leading you to your defined destination in God which he/she might have been instrumental in helping you define, by spending time with you and grooming you according to biblical principles. Janet is now in danger of losing her way trying to get back to the start point, or even if she is successful in getting her satnav, there is the danger that she does not understand the directions well enough to make the final destination. A well-versed mentor could help her stay on the right track and get to her destination much quicker.

Bringing it home, mentors in such a relationship will open the Bible and show you scriptures, and by the Spirit of God unveil revelations within, that you never even knew existed; then will go further and teach you the different ways of studying the Bible so that you do not become dependent on them but rather on the Word of God.

Action Point - Challenge:

Friends, as you study the Bible, as you grow in Christ, get yourself a mentor. Someone who will direct you and whom you can call on to ask questions from time to time. In your ministry, (whatever that may be) get a mentor that you can learn from, that will lead you by the hand and deposit things in you so that even when the mentoring relationship is over, you will have a deeper walk with Christ.

Questions for consideration when selecting a mentor:

Who is your mentor?

_____

_____

Why are you attracted to them?

_____

_____

_____

_____

Does your mentor have an obvious and plausible relationship with God and is their spiritual maturity evident?

_____

_____

_____

_____

What is their story? Where are they coming from (journey) and where are they heading (destination)?

_____

_____

_____

_____

What are the testimonies of others concerning this mentor?

_____

_____

_____

_____

Is he/she always looking for ways to grow spiritually and in all areas of life?

Yes/No*

What areas can you benefit from as a result of being under their mentorship?

_____

_____

_____

_____

Does he/she have a mentor?

Yes/No*

*A 'No' response is a cause for concern.

15. Compromised Intimacy

"So Sarai said to Abram, "The LORD has prevented me from having children. Go and sleep with my servant. Perhaps I can have children through her." And Abram agreed with Sarai's proposal."

Genesis 16:2 NLT

What a ridiculous level of compromise you might think. I will never do that, but what if I told you that this and worse still, is happening around you even as you digest the words of this devotion?

Sarai asked her maid to get intimate with her husband so that she (Sarai) could have children. I have spoken with many married women (some that I counsel), and just the fact that they caught their husbands potentially looking at another woman is a problem, let alone inciting him to do the unthinkable. Even I have had times, when I've given my husband a corresponding *'what are you looking at'* look because he dared to let his eyes wander! ☺

The truth is that the human nature, the flesh, struggles to imbibe the God kind of faith that is required to endure through the tough times when it seems God is far away, has turned His back, or is simply refusing to listen.

> *Yes, God said He would do X, Y, and Z for me, in fact He promised, and I know that His promises are yea and amen,[105] but what if I help myself out a little bit? What about having a fall-back plan in case God, sorry I mean 'I' fail? What about I have a plan B just in case I didn't quite hear God clearly, even though He has confirmed His word to me through two and three witnesses? What about I devise an alternative route, after all God understands, right? He knows that we are just human.*

Oh my!

As I consider today's text and the way we respond to life's challenges, sticking God on the back burner, and doing what feels right to us to solve our problems (by ourselves), I come to find that Sarai is not much different from many of us today, and if push comes to shove, then perhaps, we would also make such drastic decisions, and crazy concessions. We compromise on various levels and do the unthinkable sometimes even in the name of God. Then worse still, we do the same with God, we compromise our relationship with Him, as we farm out our prayers to prayer warriors and pastors to intercede on our behalf, not realising that no one can present our case to God like we can.

We contract pastors to read the word and find solutions on our behalf, and prophets to hear His voice and then regurgitate (through their various filters) the word which God wants us to hear undiluted, straight from the throne room; and thereby

---

[105] 2 Corinthians 1:20

89

elevating these men and women of God beyond where God has placed them in one's life, to the point that they become *gods, idols,* and *mini-stars* who are in competition for God's glory.

In the same way that we would not (I hope) ask another to be intimate with our spouses, we should not farm out the responsibility of worship (because prayer is a form of worship) and seeking God - to others. It's time we stopped allowing pastors, prophets, and prayer warriors to be the main channel by which we choose to hear what God is saying, but rather, allow them to confirm what God Himself has already revealed to us. It is true that at times, God may speak a word firstly through another, but we should learn to spend time communing with God so that we can discern and confirm that word which He gave; through prayer, reading the word, and spending time in His presence. Intimacy with God will birth the fruit of righteousness, but when we seek intimacy with God by sending another to be intimate on our behalf, we sow the seed of unrighteousness and reap the bitter fruit of adultery.

Let's quit delegating our relationship with God to the hands and possibly hearts of others. God cannot be mocked dear friend, what you sow is what you will reap.[106]

Action Point – Let Us Pray:

Father Lord: help me to trust You, to trust Your judgment, to stay committed to You and to know that no alternative plan will ever be able to match the plans that You have for me. Even when things get tough and trusting seems to be failing, help me to remember that You never fail. Help me not to compromise my relationship with You, but rather to yearn for a deeper level of intimacy.

---

[106] Galatians 6:7

16. The Presence of God

Then he said to Him, "If Your Presence does not go with us, do not bring us up from here. For how then will it be known that Your people and I have found grace in Your sight, except You go with us? So we shall be separate, Your people and I, from all the people who are upon the face of the earth."

Exodus 33:15-16 NKJV

The Israelites were set apart because of the presence of God that they frequently enjoyed. Moses spent a lot of time in God's presence and realised the benefit for himself and for the people of Israel. This is why he was adamant when he said to God - if your presence doesn't go with us, then we are not going.

The presence of God is essential for everyday living. We know that God is the omnipresent God. He is everywhere always and all at the same time, *(The eyes of the Lord are in every place, keeping watch on the evil and the good[107])*, but there's a special presence of God that is more than just God keeping watch over the whole world, a special reserve for those who choose to dwell habitually in His presence.

The presence I talk of is that which Moses pleaded with God for, and experienced on a regular basis, it is the presence of God which David continually desired, the presence of God which caused Elizabeth's baby to leap within her, the presence of God which was made manifest in the Man – Jesus, His name Emmanuel meaning God with us (what an awesome presence), and that same presence which we (can) enjoy today! Solomon referenced this presence of God in the book of proverbs when he encouraged the reader to acknowledge God in everything that He may direct our paths.[108]

God's presence sets us apart and keeps us hidden under His glorious realm. There, you cannot be conquered; you are more than victorious. When we make decisions, we should have the same attitude as Moses did, the same mindset that refuses to go or do anything alone, because even if you have the support of people backing you, if you don't have the presence of God, you might as well be alone. One with God is always the majority.[109]

Our constant prayer should be *"Lord if you're not in it, then I don't want to be a part of it"* or *"Lord I feel that you are leading me to do this, however, if you will not go with me, then Lord, I'm not going."*

The presence of the Lord is also a transforming agent. It gave Moses and the Israelites confidence, and a visible change was noted in Moses after he had spent

---

[107] Proverbs 15:3 ESV
[108] Proverbs 3:5-6
[109] 2 Chronicles 2:7-8

time with God. It's impossible for you to remain the same after spending time in God's presence. The transforming effect of the presence of God is permanent, leaving an indelible mark on the tablet of your heart. When the angel of the Lord first appeared to Gideon under the Ophrah tree, Gideon was a weakling, but before long, the effect of the time spent in God's presence was evident as the spirit of God engulfed him and he became victorious.[110]

The same can be said of Moses, whose face shone brightly after an encounter with God, such that men could not look upon Him.[111] An encounter with God sets you apart. People see you, but more than that they see the God in you and acknowledge His presence in your life (Abraham).[112]

Nowadays people find it difficult to encounter God in the way that those of ages past did, but God's presence will only be as close and as real to us as we want Him to be, and that starts by spending time in and with the Living Word. The truth is that the flesh is not interested in an encounter with God and sometimes even the soul is weary. Engaging the spirit of man is the key to connecting with the Spirit of God, so that man (spirit, soul, and body) becomes alive and sensitive to God's presence; we can achieve this by speaking to the soul,[113] and feeding the spirit with the word of God.

Action Point - Let Us Pray:

- Father Lord, thank You for Your presence that covers the whole world. Thank You because You are always there. I thank You especially because Your presence is as real as the air that I breathe. Thank You for setting me apart to enjoy Your presence on a level that is humanly impossible to explain.

- Lord I pray that I will continually be drawn to You, and that I will yield to You my heart, soul, and spirit, so that You may transform them. When people see me, let them see the God in me, let them see You. Hide me in Your glorious realm; keep me safe by the pillar of cloud by day and the pillar of fire by night, just as You did with the Israelites.

- May I continually enjoy the sweetness and benefits of Your presence and may Your words perpetually be engraved on my heart in Jesus name. Amen.

God is near to those who are near to Him. Seek Him out. He's closer than you think. You'll find that He's actually the one drawing you to Him, seeking the true, spirit-filled worshipper in you.

---

[110] Judges 6-7
[111] Exodus 34:29-30
[112] Genesis 21:22
[113] Psalm 103:1

17. Praying with Purpose

"And when you pray, do not use vain repetitions as the heathen do. For they think that they will be heard for their many words."

Matthew 6:7 NKJV

Anytime of any day, the devil would rather you made plans that don't include God than those which do. So much so that in this day and age, we are in a rush to do everything quickly, right from the moment we wake up till the time we go to bed; we are so busy that we hardly remember God in our day. If He's at all lucky we might murmur a recital of a prayer in the morning, or some other form of words jumbled together, with absolutely no thought about what they mean and with no real structure to our words in prayer, or our request, or our praise and offering of worship to God.

I have found myself in this position quite a lot in the past and God knows I have been working at getting better by working on maintaining a communication line consistently throughout the day. As an example, I will engage in conversation with God in the most random topics at intervals during the day (I love how humorous God can be sometimes).

When I was younger, I remember learning how to pray. Once we were able to string some sentences into meaningful paragraphs of prayer (which we would utter when called upon to pray) we then had a sure 'winning formula' that became our blueprint and creed for every time we were called upon to pray - the words of that prayer hardly changed. That might have been good for a child or for one just learning how to pray, but as the Christian matures, it is expected that his or her prayer style and communication habits would also mature.

As my children were growing up, I noticed the same trait in them; their prayers were more or less the same, day after day with no real meaning to it. I was getting bored listening in, and I'm almost 99% sure God was too, imagine having the same conversation every day with your loved ones like it was 'groundhog day' ☺

So I said to my children, *pray with purpose* and this is what I meant and taught them:

Think about your day: the difficult and easy tasks you expect to meet along the way; the people that you will meet; how you expect to make an impact, excel, and display excellence; then structure these into your prayer. Look for and use related scriptures and promises and add these to your prayer. Given that we are in and developing a relationship with God (it's not like we're dating right?), be informal, be free. Use everyday language, use layman terms: *you are not King James*. God is not interested in the eloquence of your speech, He understands every language from street slang to the Queens English, from the tears we cry to the joyful laughter.

I encourage you, dear reader, to pray with purpose. Bring God into every facet of life as your words structure your prayer, and then listen for what His response will be. You might be surprised by some of the minute information that He is interested in.

Next, I encourage you to confabulate with God continually throughout the day. This is a habit that needs to be formed and one that requires a conscious effort.

Consider this:

> *Some people asked Smith Wigglesworth, a great Apostle of Faith in the first half of the 20th century, about prayer. They said, "Smith Wigglesworth, you're a man of faith and miracles, you've raised people from the dead. You've cast out more demons than we've had hot dinners. Tell us, how long do you pray every day?"*
>
> *"Well," the apostle replied, "I don't ever pray any longer than twenty minutes.*
>
> *"What?" his questioners exclaimed. After pausing for effect, Smith Wigglesworth continued, "Yes, but I never go twenty minutes without praying".*

Your prayer life is not measured in minutes. Prayer is a lifestyle. Prayer is a constant two-way communication with God. Prayer is essential to living in freedom.

When we involve God in everything, from the minor to the major, the simplicities and also the intricate details of life, then our plans will be aligned to His ultimate plans as He guides and leads us, and His will, will be done in our lives.

When we commit everything into His hands, we don't need to worry. There's a Yoruba proverb, which says that *the plate you place in God's hand never breaks, and the cloth you give to Him never gets torn*, so, whatever you give and surrender wholeheartedly to God is secure and sorted. Oh yes, the enemy will come with lies and cerebrations that will seek to trigger worry, inject distress, and activate doubt and fear, which could lead you into thinking that God is not involved, and thereby instigating an illusion which suggests that God's hands are tied or that He is limited, but my questions to you are: whose report do you believe? Is God able to do exceedingly, abundantly above all that you ask or think, according to His power that is at work in your life?

Speak to God about your today and do that every single day, and know that your tomorrow, your future is sorted when you build your foundation in Christ today.

Action Point - Activities:

Ponder upon these points from today's devotion:

1. Praying with purpose takes the intricate details of your day into account; with God everything matters.

2. God is not interested in the eloquence of your speech; He understands every language from the tears we cry, the groans we make to the joyful laughter.

3. You are in a relationship with God, so start acting like that when you talk to Him and stop behaving like it's a formal interview.

18. Trusting Love

He came to His own, and His own did not receive Him.

John 1:11 NKJV

A couple of years ago, I met with a friend to discuss plans for her upcoming wedding. As you do, we started talking about love and what love really means, and soon enough, we were talking about suspicion; not so much the suspicion where our partners were concerned but more so with friends, and how we kept the so called 'friends' at arm's length because of the potential damage they may (or perhaps will) cause; the heartbreak that will ensue and tears at the end of the day, but as we took the discourse further, we started considering the chances that sometimes we were the cause of the heartache in the first place. Why? Because we don't trust love!!!

The outcome of not trusting love and allowing suspicion to breed on the beds of our hearts results in suspecting genuine love and presenting one hundred other reasons for our suspicion, instead of allowing love to prevail.

Now, this is understandable, especially if we haven't come from a very loving background or perhaps we just haven't experienced true love - *but* when we come to understand and experience the joy that the love of God brings, the God that is love, and when we allow our hearts to mature with that love and in love; then not only do we overcome that often false suspicion which seeks to replace genuine love, we strive to be an emblem, a reflection of that love.

And you know what? I've come to find that love attracts love! When you 'become' love by expressing love and choosing to love, then other people around you begin to replicate and reflect that love; I call it contagious love. It's true that there will be freeloaders along the way, there always are; those who will use and maybe even abuse you, but the Bible[114] says *"love keeps no record or wrong" (NLT)*, or *"love knows no evil" (NKJV)*. Even when we are cheated, the proceeds and benefits of love and loving others far outweigh having a suspicious mind.

The Bible encourages us to accept wrong and allow ourselves to be cheated,[115] I'm serious - go check it out. And when you think about it, Jesus went through a lot more. When we have the mindset of love, regardless of the fact that that love might be defrauded, we will keep on moving on whether wronged or not; cheated or not; and the enemy will truly be defeated.

Most times our suspicions are wrong; they are just evil thoughts, which the enemy has planted to trouble our minds, distract us, and steal our joy. Even Jesus came to His own people and they did not receive Him; they were probably thinking *'what*

---

[114] 1 Corinthians 13:5
[115] 1 Corinthians 6:7

can this carpenter boy do for us? We knew him from when he was a toddler' - and so their suspicion robbed them of first-hand (spiritual and physical) miracles and blessings.

The book of 1ˢᵗ Corinthians,[116] in its definition of love, tells us that love thinks no evil; this means it is always thinking the best in every situation, some might refer to it as *positive thinking* but I'd take that a step further to say *positive thinking with the mindset of Christ*. This doesn't mean we become a doormat, but when we display this character, God will increase our wisdom in dealing with certain situations in love.

Suspicion is dangerous and has wrecked many marriages and relationships. If your mind is troubled, the best thing to do is to give that troubled mind over to the Lord in prayer, asking God to attend to and deal with the situation, and to take the negative feeling away. Furthermore, we should not go around trying to evidence suspicion, that's just a waste of precious time and that's what the devil wants us to do.

Action Point - Let Us Pray

Father Lord, help me to deal with every suspicious mindset that I might have (or that has been troubling me), especially when there is no basis for it and I have simply conjured, or allowed the enemy to fill my mind with negative emotions. Help me to always love first and to choose love over suspicion every single time. Help me to break free from the spirit of suspicion. I pray that your Spirit will reside in me, and that my mind will be filled with positive things, Jesus things!!! In Jesus name I pray, Amen.

---

[116] 1 Corinthians 13:5

19. The Possibility of Holiness

For the scriptures say, 'You must be holy because I am holy.'

1 Peter 1:16 NLT

Sometimes, we see holiness as a really high level that only monks, nuns, priests, pastors (or those in solitary confinement) can attain. In fact, we give excuses and reasons why we can't be holy or live a holy life.

We say:

'I'm only human' 'I'm limited'   *'I'm full of sin'*   *'I'm not God'*

'Man's heart is evil' and 'I am unclean and my righteousness filthy like dirty rags'

We forget that in order to come before the One that is holy, holiness is required,[117] and holiness is certainly possible. It is no longer like it used to be in the Old Testament, when men had to be more conscious about cleansing activities, religious rites, and rituals before approaching God; He bids us to come as we are so that He can cleanse us like no ram or bull ever can.

When we experience the presence of God, the reality of who we are, our filth, and our unrighteousness is exposed to us as the Holy Spirit, the Spirit of God that is *Holy*, convicts us and then by the blood of Jesus (already shed for us) cleanses us.[118] God continually draws us unto Himself[119] because He loves us and wants us to be holy, in response to such great love, it is then for us to remain holy and to remain in Him.

Many times, in life we are afraid to live holy because it separates us from the world and the truth be told, many of us don't want to be separate from the world. We love the attention of the world and the platforms and pedestal both the world and the *church* afford us. We chorus that we must go where they are (the world) to help them see the light of God that we carry, but how is that even possible when we don't go with fire, when our light is dim and nearly out? We allow the world to blow out the candle of light God has given us and at times we are even instrumental in giving the world a helping hand to switch on the fan that will extinguish our light/fire; it is questionable if indeed we are salt in this world,[120] if we get our sweetness from the world.

Holiness in and of itself is a separation from sin, from flesh unto God. However, holiness is not complete simply because we choose to separate ourselves from sin; holiness in all its totality is when we then take the next step and choose to be separated unto God. Holiness can be defined in one word - *obedience*. It is when

[117] Psalm 24:2-3
[118] Isaiah 6:1,5
[119] John 6:44
[120] Matthew 5:13

we make a conscious effort to live by the standards and the dictates of the word of God; ambassadors of Christ and citizens of the Kingdom of God, here on earth. It is God's desire for us to turn away from sin and to depend upon, have total reliance, and trust in Him. He sent Jesus Christ, His only Son to die for us, so that we may be set free from the bondage of sin and live a life of abundance, a life in eternity with Him.

So how can we be holy? See the action points that follow:

Action Points - Reflections:

- Understand that it is the Holy Spirit that enables you to be holy. The simple truth is that you cannot be holy by your own effort, the flesh can never be holy, it constantly wages war against holiness; but by the infilling, power, and leading of the Holy Spirit *you can be holy*.

- Be intentional about living holy. Obedience is key. Accept that regardless of who you are or what you have done, holiness is possible because we serve a God who can make the seemingly impossible - possible. Living a holy life doesn't mean that we do not sin, but rather that we choose *not* to sin and deliberately stay away from habitual sin.

- Acknowledge that you are in the world but not of the world. You are difference. Seek to influence the world by the Spirit of God and His principles, rather than to be influenced by the world and its standards.

- Surround yourself with other believers who have chosen to live and be committed to a lifestyle which promotes holiness. Such friends will keep you in check, they are your accountability siblings in Christ, correcting you when you err, yet encouraging you every day in your Christian walk and pursuit of holiness.

- Expose your heart to the word of God, don't hide and say certain scripture is not for you (especially the ones that doesn't suit your questionable lifestyle). Allow it to prick your heart, to transform your mind. Only be conscious of the world around you and be careful not to conform to it.

- Shine the light of God everywhere you go. Do not allow the world to quench the fire of God inside of you.

- Continually offer yourself as a living sacrifice, remembering that a sacrifice is for the slaughter. You may be living but be alive to the Spirit of God at work in you and dead to worldly pursuits and sinful desires. It's not going to be a bed of roses, but the end is sure going to be much sweeter than the beginning.

20. In His Image

He is the image of the invisible God,
the firstborn over all creation.

Colossians 1:15 NKJV

God created everything according to its *kind*. Man is the only creation made in the likeness of God,[121] even though man was God's last creations. Mankind can therefore be called *Godkind*.

Right from the beginning, God purposed that man would be set apart, different from all the other things that He made. God loved man so much that He gave him power and authority (even over those things that were created before him, and that includes the angels). In this way, God sends a clear message to man and to all creation that man is special; we are a chosen people, a royal priesthood, a holy nation, a peculiar people[122] set apart from the world that we live in and set unto Him.

It would take years, decades, maybe even centuries for man to fully grasp this truth if at all, but God, the Master Planner had this in mind from the very beginning, well before creation.[123]

The truth that God chooses to love us this way, and set us apart specially, is not something we should take lightly. When we explore all creatures, we will find that they are all *fit for the purpose* for which they were created and behave according to their kind. So much so that abnormal creatures can be ostracised, given up for research and experiments, or even killed.

We lost our identity and our image after the likeness of God, when we allowed / allow the enemy to distort our image. It's almost like he took away that perfectly clean, pristine mirror which we look through to see God's image and reflection and switched it with those distorted mirrors that we see at the funfair. And we let him! Our continuous thirst to be different from what God created us to be so that we can fit into the world around us started long ago in the Garden of Eden, and has consequently switched our image and identity, and left us completely misguided.

Adam and Eve sought to be like God, but they missed the truth that they already looked like Him, and their desire for something else caused them to sin and step outside of God's perfect plan. Their dissatisfaction crippled their destiny and left mankind chasing all sorts of shadows. Even today, we see dissatisfied men and women experimenting with all sorts of things outside of God; men change their sex wanting to experience life as a woman for no viable reason at all and vice versa, and

---

[121] Genesis 1:27
[122] 1 Peter 2:9
[123] Jeremiah 1:5

dissatisfied people resort to plastic surgery, not for medical reasons but to reconstruct what God has beautifully knitted together, calling to question His initial design.

God's image is perfect. He wants us to be perfect just like He is perfect[124] and this is why He created us in His image, because that was the best option for mankind.

Jesus Himself is the visible image of the invisible God.[125] In Him we see the true image and nature of all that God created, purposed and designed for us to be. Jesus came to die for our sins, to restore us, to take and smash the distorted mirror in exchange for that perfect, pristine mirror, so that once again, we can look like God. Are you holding tightly to that distorted mirror, or are you having too much fun in the funfair of the world and refusing to let go? In His image is the *BEST* you will ever be; refuse to listen to the lies of the enemy, there's nothing more outside of God. The mirror the enemy presents you with is a façade; look properly and you will see that it's not perfect, it is not the truth.

Action Point - Let Us Pray

Heavenly Father, thank You for creating me in Your image and then affording me the opportunity to be restored to Your likeness (through Jesus) even after the fall of man. Help me to see that You have made me perfectly and that being in Your likeness is the best that I can ever be. Help me to be satisfied with this truth and to yearn daily to be more like You, to be continually drawn to You. Thank You because I know that You have answered. In Jesus name I pray. Amen.

---

[124] Matthew 5:48
[125] Colossians 1:15

Emerge

~ Bonuses ~

1. To Worship You I Live

And Abraham said to his young men, "Stay here with the donkey;
the lad and I will go yonder and worship, and we will come back to you."

Gen 22:5 NKJV

Worship belongs to God and God alone. Genesis 22 presents the first time that we come across the word worship; in this case, worship was about to be offered unto God.

Abraham lived a life of worship. Although this is the first time we hear/read the word worship; I think it goes without saying that this was *not* the first time that Abraham would worship God. We can deduce that it was very likely that worshipping God was part of his nature, part of who he was, so when asked where he was going, his response came naturally.

Reading chapter 22 in full, we find that worship requires preparation.[126] Abraham had everything he needed to worship God; we do not read that he got to the top of the mountain before remembering. In the same way, we must be prepared to worship God daily. We can do this by spending time with Him, listening to Him, and following His leading.

Worship requires obedience;[127] we could even say worship is obedience. It is a lie and a misnomer to state confidently that we are living the life of worship if our behaviour, character, and nature are not lined up in obedience to the word of God.

Worship is a sacrifice! Abraham was on his way to sacrifice his son. This means that if our worship is convenient for us, if it doesn't cost us, then it is not worship; worship happens outside of our comfort zone. Worship must be offered to God both when we are personally motivated to do so, and even when all the odds are stacked against us, and it is painful to do so.

To worship is to give life. Abraham went to give the life of his *only son* to God, just like Hannah later dedicated her son to the Lord, in the same way Jesus came to this world to die for us.[128] Our sacrifice to God is not complete if we only give part of our lives, we must give our lives completely as a living sacrifice.

Worship is giving!!! Abraham went to give, not to receive. Even though he was giving away his most *'prized possession'* that he had longed for and waited years for, he didn't complain. Too often, we worship God for what He has done or is doing, as we expect Him to do. We confuse worship with thanksgiving or even praise. Worship is done in spite of challenging circumstances.

---

[126] Genesis 22:3
[127] Genesis 22:2, 10
[128] John 3:16

104

Action Point - Reflection:

- Consider the steps you take when you are intentional about worshipping God; are you always prepared? What changes can you make to change how you worship God?

- Worship requires obedience. There are many things that we would rather do our way than the way that is pleasing to God. Consider areas of your life where your preferences have taken priority over God's direct instructions to you; how can you make changes to be obedient to the word of God?

- Abraham was willing to turn over his only son as a love exchange, in obedience to the voice of God. Equally, God gave His Son, Jesus, as a love exchange that we may be reconciled to Him. These are significant sacrifices. How can your worship to God be more sacrificial?

- What is your most prized possession on earth? Can you give this up in a flash if God required it of you? Pray and ask God to work on your heart to be more obedient and responsive to His voice. Pray that God will help you to worship Him in Spirit and in truth, and in a way that is pleasing to Him.

Debbie Akinkunle

2. The Radiance of God

"When Moses came down Mount Sinai carrying the two stone tablets inscribed with the terms of the covenant, he wasn't aware that his face had become radiant because he had spoken to the Lord. So when Aaron and the people of Israel saw the radiance of Moses' face, they were afraid to come near him."

Exodus 34:29-30 NLT

We live in a society where we sometimes forget who we are due to the trials, tribulations, and chaos that surround us. Sometimes, due to the affairs of the world and the things we go through in our personal lives, our faith and trust in God are shaken, and sometimes this makes us compromise.

1 Corinthians 7:23 (NLT) states that "God paid a high price for you, so don't be enslaved by the world." In the world today; we sometimes do the opposite and become enslaved and forget the high price God paid for us when Jesus Christ died on the cross of Calvary; sometimes the source of our enslavement could be our jobs, friends, family, or peers; all these things hinder us from becoming intimate with God.

Sometimes, we walk the surface of the earth yet people do not see the glory of God in our lives. When Moses went up Mount Sinai and spent time with God, the people of Israel saw that his face was radiant (he wasn't even aware of this) and they were afraid to go near him because the glory of Yahweh was radiating through him.

From Moses we learn that as believers, we are to proclaim God's glory. Our lives are supposed to be transformed by God; Matthew 17:1-8 talks of the transformation of our Lord Jesus Christ that took place on Mount Tabor. God wants our lives to proclaim His glory so that the world can see; when we chase the proclamation and radiance of God and seek the Kingdom of Heaven first, the riches of the world will follow.

Matthew 6:33 says *"But seek ye first the kingdom of God, and his righteousness; and all these things shall be added unto you."* When our lives proclaim God's glory, we are eligible for His kingdom which is why it is very important to submit to the Lord, the Potter, because when we do, we will live to please Him and we will be empowered to close our eyes to things of the world and open our minds to chase the Kingdom of God wholeheartedly.

Action Point – Let Us Pray:

Father, I run into Your loving arms because you own me: You created me, and nothing can separate me from Your love. At this moment, I pray, let my life radiate Your glory because You are the God who gave Moses the grace for the world to see Your glory in him. I am praying you let the world see Your glory in me.

Isaiah 60:1 states "Arise, shine; for thy light is come, and the glory of the Lord is risen upon thee." I am praying You let Your glory be risen upon me, my life, my

106

home, my marriage, my education, my job, my family, my children, and more. I pray Your power fills me; send down your Paraclete which is the Holy Spirit to show me the way. I pray that You let me live a life that will please You and You alone, I am praying that You transform me just like Jesus was transformed in front of James, Peter, and John on Mount Tabor. This and many more I ask for in Jesus name I pray. Amen.

Taiwo Jabita

3. Outliving The Flesh

*"...I'm landing punches on my own body
and subduing it like a slave..."*

1 Corinthians 9:27 CEB

The idea of crucifying the flesh is poignant and significant in relation to the crucifixion of Jesus Christ[129] and how He physically died to show us what must be done (with our flesh). Whilst the death of our flesh is not expected to be as brutal nor as 'real' as Christ's, it certainly helps us to appreciate the death and resurrection of our Lord and Saviour; and for the purpose of this devotion, helps us to understand that whilst we discipline our flesh here on earth for the benefit of the spirit, the latter is greater and will last through eternity. It is better for us to suffer but for a while, whilst here on earth in exchange for a glorious eternal future with Jesus.[130]

People tend to view the extremities of crucifying the flesh as impossible but this can be achieved, even by little *acts,* such as turning down something that doesn't fit into ones meal plan and substituting it for something that fits, goes a long way into crucifying the flesh and of course, there is the added benefit of looking after and treating our temple right; and so just from this one little *act,* we can achieve both physical and spiritual benefits.

Crucifying the flesh helps us to avoid nature's sinful passions and desires, choosing to do the right thing, that which serves and glorifies the Lord and not something that is self-exalting or self-exhilarating.

Many people have stories about how they've tried to do things their way or have asked for the help from others before eventually turning to God, they testify that it is only when they remembered God and turned to Him that things took a turn for the better.[131] It is only after repenting from our impatience and lack of trust in God, and then turning back to Him from our 'brief visits to the world' that it becomes clearer that the problems we faced could have been resolved much sooner and heartaches suffered less if we had held unto our faith in God throughout the process. It is time to overcome our earthly shell and slide back to God (and not backslide from Him).[132]

One of the greatest mistakes people make while lavishing in worldly pleasures is claiming that they'll go back to God once they've finished enjoying or living out their sin; others make mistakes by only calling on God when they are in dire need of His help; still others believe that they are safe so long as they are living a *good* life. This is dangerous - why risk eternal life for a potential tomorrow that is not guaranteed?

---

[129] Matthew 27:32-56
[130] 1 Peter 5:10
[131] Proverbs 3:7
[132] Proverbs 3:5-8

The truth, which all will eventually realise is that no matter how many false victories man may claim in himself, God always wins. No, scratch that, God has already won.[133]

Action Point – Let Us Pray:

Lord Jesus, remind us daily that You are our winner, You have won for us and You have been crucified for us. I pray that we are replenished and renewed daily by Your Spirit. Help us to remain strong in our faith and to cling unto You. We thank You for Your love and for continuously taking us back. We are grateful for Your mercy. Thank You Lord. Amen

Precious Monique Akinkunle

---

[133] Daniel 4:25

4. Righteousness a Gift!

He shall receive blessing from the Lord,
and righteousness from the God of his salvation.

Psalm 24:5 NKJV

This scripture makes it clear that righteousness is a gift, available to you and I, which comes about from obedience and holiness (two synonymous words)!

Some may say: *"God is gracious and merciful; perhaps I can just stand in line to receive righteousness or maybe if I attend church regularly and pray for the gift of righteousness, I will receive it".*

Well, let's take a closer look into Psalm 24. What does it say about the requirements for this gift?

The preceding verses identifies the prerequisites for righteousness as clean hands and a pure heart; attached with watching what you say and do, by not swearing deceitfully or not regarding things of iniquity or vanity, i.e. idols or materialistic things.

Who may ascend into the hill of the Lord? Or who may stand in His holy place?
He who has clean hands and a pure heart, who has not lifted up his soul to an idol,
nor sworn deceitfully[134]

Grace is also a requirement since the Bible makes it clear that the righteousness of man is like a filthy rag[135] and the heart of man is desperately wicked.[136] Therefore, man's heart cannot of its own accord become pure as in verse 4 of Psalm 24, it takes the grace of God.

The truth about grace is that it will not just come and smack you in the face, neither can you just pray for grace, sit back and expect grace to abound and righteousness to follow.

God wants us to be holy and to receive the gift of righteousness; but you have to actively seek it. 'Actively' being the key word here which requires us to make a conscious decision and effort to seek out righteousness, to find out what it is, what the requirements are, and then to go hard after it. In seeking righteousness, you'll find that a number of other unexpected blessings will follow. Matthew 6:33 is not limited to material blessings either, Romans 5:17 (b) gives us a deeper insight into the everlasting blessing that the believer receives upon accepting the gift of righteousness.

But even greater is God's wonderful grace and his gift of righteousness, for all who receive it will live in triumph over sin and death through this one man, Jesus Christ.

---

[134] Psalm 24:3-4 NKJV
[135] Isaiah 64:6
[136] Jeremiah 17:9

Action Point - Let Us Pray:

Father thank You for the gift of Your grace, which is available to me, through Your Son Jesus Christ, who died that I might live and triumph over sin. Help me to understand the gift of Your righteousness, to seek after it ardently and to openly receive it. Purify me, cleanse my lips, and help me to stay pure.

Help me to live a life that pleases You.

Debbie Akinkunle

5. The Mind is a Battlefield

Do not fret or have any anxiety about anything, but in every circumstance and in everything, by prayer and petition (definite requests), with thanksgiving, continue to make your wants known to God.

And the God's peace [shall be yours, that tranquil state of a soul assured of its salvation through Christ, and so fearing nothing from God and being content with its earthly lot of whatever sort that is, that peace], which transcends all understanding, shall garrison and mount guard over your hearts and minds in Christ Jesus.

For the rest, brethren, whatever is true, whatever is worthy of reverence and is honourable and seemly, whatever is just, whatever is pure, whatever is lovely and lovable, whatever is kind and winsome and gracious, if there is any virtue and excellence, if there is anything worthy of praise, think on and weigh and take account of these things [fix your minds on them].

Philippians 4:6-8 AMPC

As humans, our hearts are always under constant attack by the enemy, and challenged by the issues of life, because they are exposed to all sorts of things. That's why Paul in verse 8 of our Bible reading warns us to always think of or about things that are pure, lovely and lovable, kind and winsome and gracious, because these thoughts help keep our heart in check and free from a heart attack.

I remember a year ago, I found myself in a difficult and dark situation and it seemed as if there was no way out at all. Isn't it funny that when you are in a situation like that, a bleak moment in life, the devil comes to have a field day with you and prey on your weakness?

One night I was sitting on the bed in deep thoughts and I was asking God "Why me?" Interesting how we ask those kinds of questions when all is not going too well for us, right? At some point I think I was depressed. Different thoughts began to flood my mind and I heard them *clearly; "Does God really love you, with all you do for Him, see how He repays you, you are not loved by anyone, you are on your own, why don't you just kill yourself? (Yes you read right). You might as well just forget about this God."*

Thank God that I was able to grab a hold of my thoughts and all of a sudden I called myself back from such thoughts. I switched and began to praise God from that point onwards, I got an assurance from God as I engaged my spirit and I held on to the words He gave me with my life.

In this season of your life, God has a word for You too!

I've come to find that when you give space or allowance for the mind to be freely invaded by anything, the devil will begin to throw things at you from all directions to try to get you down and ultimately to destroy you. He will do what he can to steal your joy, kill your dreams, and destroy your destiny.

Proverbs 4:23 (AMPC) says:

> *Keep and guard your heart with all vigilance and above*
> *all that you guard, for out of it flows the springs of life.*

In a nutshell, Solomon, in the above scripture warns us to guard our hearts with all vigilance (meaning to be very watchful about what comes into our hearts) because out of the heart, flows the issues of life. The Bible says, as a man thinketh, so is he. So, think and set your mind on good things.

Action Point – Let Us Pray:

Lord, help me and teach me to guard my heart with all diligence. Help me to think on things that please You alone.

Tope Ajewole

6. The Power of Sharing

We've all heard the phrase *'a problem shared is a problem halved'*. You may consider this a very true and powerful statement, but let's take this phrase one step further and say, *'A testimony shared, is another person blessed'*.

Now consider and keep the following passage in mind from Mark 5:19 NLT:

But Jesus said,

"No, go home to your family, and tell them everything the Lord has done for you and how merciful he has been."

A testimony in a religious context can be defined as a public recounting of a religious conversion or experience. For example, speaking to a friend, or group of friends about something you believe God has done for you.

The first Sunday of the month (otherwise known as Thanksgiving Sunday at my church) is one of my favourites. Why? Simply because for the best part of an hour, the church gets to listen to, and be blessed by the testimonies of others as they talk of how God has been actively moving in their lives. We learn about the miracles, favour, and turnarounds that these individuals have experienced in their lives.

There are two main and very simple reasons why there is power in sharing your testimony:

First and foremost, it's what Jesus repeatedly told the people He healed in the New Testament to do. Take a look at Mark 5:19 again. Before this verse, we read that Jesus had just performed a miracle relieving (delivering) a man of a demon he possessed. Upon his freedom from bondage, the delivered man REALLY wanted to follow after Jesus, but he did not allow him. Instead, Jesus told him to go and tell others what had happened. When God does something for you, it's not only for you. You certainly shouldn't just sit on it and keep it a secret, because that achieves no purpose. It's unfair to keep it a secret when you can use it to be a blessing to others.

This second point is that when we share what the Lord has done for us with others, it encourages them and goes a long way to strengthen their faith. Luke 8:16 says: "No one after lighting a lamp covers it with a jar or puts it under a bed, but puts it on a stand, so that those who enter may see the light". I like the analogy used here and I think it can also be applied to the topic of sharing testimonies. When something miraculous happens to you, telling others will encourage them, inspire them, and uplift them. Imagine you are about to take a test but statistics show, and you heard that multiple people fail first time around; suddenly, someone from your church comes to you and tells you that God has helped him/her to score 96% on the test first time around. Will that not encourage you? Will you not believe that God can do the same for you too? Will it not make the test seem less daunting and perhaps, even easier? That's the power of a testimony! When you hear that it is not possible and yet it happened to someone else, you'll get excited and encouraged because God is still in the business of turning people's lives and situations around.

So, dearly beloved, these are just two reasons why it's important to share your testimony. There are no benefits in keeping the good news and testament of what God has done in your life a secret, it doesn't help anybody. Rather, share your experience with others; they will bless them immensely. This is also a simple way to evangelise and tell of God's goodness.

Keep sharing!

Sinmi Soroye

7. The Mask

For those who live according to the flesh set their minds on the things of the flesh, but those who live according to the Spirit set their minds on the things of the Spirit.

Romans 8:5 ESV

Everyone has a mask that they wear, some just know how to make their mask look real. It's so easy to compare our lives to the next person. It's a habit that has been mastered by many since childhood. Few overcome it; some control it, while others drown in it! As technology advances, comparison is becoming like a strong mudslide, taking down anyone who dares to remain in its surroundings. We compare our lives to those on television, in magazines, on the runway, and on social media.

I did the 'comparison thing' for many years and really had to pull myself out of it. Growing up, I adored Whitney Houston! She was my "idol". I would watch her on stage while she danced and sang, and I often would imagine myself on stage doing the same thing. Whitney had an amazing voice, a voice every young girl listening and watching wanted and every performance she gave was 110%! In my eyes, Whitney Houston could do no wrong. She was the perfect role model. Around 2005, I began to hear rumours about Whitney being on drugs! Those rumours really upset me and made me angry. I wondered why people would be so wicked and make up such lies about such a wonderful woman. The media is just trying to ruin her reputation, I thought. For many years I still refused to believe it, until it all became evident that doubtlessly, Whitney had a problem, a drug problem.

I wondered how she managed to hide it for so long, or was it simply that I was blinded by what I wanted to believe. I witnessed many other celebrities, or others in the limelight being exposed for similar experiences; from drug and alcohol abuse, infidelity, to depression, identity crises, insecurities, physical abuse.

We know these issues too well, because even though we are not in the limelight, we also have, or know someone who has had similar experiences. But, there is one thing that we all have in common: the mask!

I remember someone saying to me, 'your life is so perfect' and in my head, my response was 'if only you knew'. I would faithfully get up in the mornings; get ready to leave the house but stopping along the way to pick the items I needed for the day and of course, my mask. I used the mask when I was in high school, in front of bullies; when I had to sing in front of a large crowd; and when I got in trouble. It didn't stop there either, I put the mask on when I had to attend an interview, or when I was confronted with an uncomfortable situation, or when I was going through pain but still had to put on a front and be at work.

The truth is that to some degree, we all have our personal masks that we wear, but we also forget that others have theirs too. Just log onto any of the major social media platforms to see what I mean. You will see a whole load of masks, and no, I'm not

116

talking about makeup, lol. I'm talking about people using pictures, videos, and other forms of messages to hide their pain, their hurt, even who they really are.

Tell me: when was the last time that you saw someone take a selfie while crying? When was the last time you saw a couple in a picture reveal their dysfunction? Very few people want others to know what they are going through. Very few give others access into their real world. Most just put on a mask and pretend like everything is great. I'm sure you're wondering what's my point in all this, right?

My point is - stop comparing your life to the façade of someone else. Don't allow the pictures of others to mislead you into the life that you think everyone else is living but you! Realize that many wear masks to hide the truth, while others have found a way to deal with their shortcomings and live happy lives.

I've learned to deal with mine. You want to know my secret? His name is Jesus. He helps me to remove the pain and live a life that pleases Him. He helps me to take the focus off myself and the opinion of others so that I don't have to keep reaching for the mask. Yes, there are still times when I will go through difficult times, times of pain, times of confusion but as long as I lean on Jesus, I know I will be alright, my help truly comes from the Lord. (Psalm 121:2)

Action Point - Prayer:

To You I give my life, oh Lord. Help me to focus on You. Keep me from the distractions of the world. Remind me to chase after the treasures of heaven and not the pleasures of the world. Help me to be honest and transparent in all my doings. Help me to live the life you have destined for me, rather than reaching for the mask every time. Thank You for always being there for me and being a true friend that I can always lean on. I love You majorly.

Mercy Fakoya

8. New Season Shift

*"And when the devil had ended all the temptation,
he departed from him for a season."*

Luke 4:13 KJV

As nature's season's change, so also do the seasons of our lives. However, God's love never changes; He is with us through every season of our lives.

Life is very seasonal

By God's design, life happens in seasons. Each season is unique and comes with both its challenges and blessings. We often find ourselves in difficult situations and we sometimes feel all alone in those seasons. The Bible, however, is filled with stories of those who walked with God through such seasons; Job will be a perfect example. He lost everything and it seemed at some point that he lost God too. When we feel lost, we can find direction and peace in knowing that no matter the season, God is relentless in His love, grace, and mercy toward us.

Grow into your new season

It took 40 years of wilderness wandering before the Israelites walked into the Promised Land. David was a shepherd for years before he became King. Sarah was barren for 90 years before she became the mother of nations. The woman with the issue of blood searched for 12 years before being healed. All these people went through seasons, which encouraged their growth, and elevated them to new seasons.

A new season comes with new challenges and enemies. Sometimes, when you ask God for a promotion, He will schedule an adversary. The presence of an enemy could be a sign of an exit from one season and entry to another. When it was time for God to move David into his new season of kingship, Goliath showed up.[137] When Joseph was close to stepping into his new season as Governor of Egypt, Potiphar's wife appeared.[138] Such wars, battles, challenges, and new enemies are indicators of a pending new season in your life. At such times, spiritual attacks come in waves and this is evident in today's scripture.

In those times, I never pray to God that the challenges be taken away; I just pray and ask God for strength. And sooner or later, the season passes. When you delay a battle, you delay your reward. If David had delayed the battle with Goliath or run away from it, he may never have been a king. When Jesus was about to step into a new season after fasting for 40 days and 40 nights, the devil showed up and tempted him using his current state of hunger and need for food. But Jesus knew that the

---

[137] 1 Samuel 17:6-22
[138] Genesis 39

enemy always stands at the exit of one season to stop you from going out, and at the entrance of another season to stop you from going in. Remember, the appearance of a new enemy or battle could be a sign of an exit from one season and entry to a new season.

Action Point – Let Us Pray:

Thank You Father for every season that I have experienced in life because I now understand that each season is a weapon that I will use to conquer the next. Teach me Lord to embrace the seasons as they come and give me the strength to stand strong in the tornadoes of life. Strengthen my faith and my spirit; Lord, I trust You and I know that with You I cannot sink.

Amen.

Daniel Babalola

9. Worthy

"I cried out, "I am slipping" but your unfailing love, O lord, supported me. When doubt filled my mind, your comfort gave me renewed hope and cheer"

Psalm 94:18-19 NLT

The only thing that I can hear is silence, pure silence. No more noise, no more shouting, "I will turn you into nothing" Oh! But I feel the anger burning in my soul, making my heartache. I want to punch a wall; better still, I really want to break something. I want to take away this aching pain in my heart. Why do I feel so much pain? Why am I crying? Why do I believe them when they say that I am unworthy? Why is no one fighting for me? Who is on my side? Do I really belong here? Why am I still on earth? God, why don't they like me? Why am I always wrong? I give my all, why is that never enough? *WHY AM I NOT ENOUGH?* Useless? Insignificant? Failure? Irrelevant? Pointless? Rude? Too holy? Too churchy? Why am I a know-it-all? Why am I unworthy?

I don't know who you are, but I know that at some point you have been made to feel so unworthy by others. You have been called names because you have chosen to live a life devoted to God.

- At some point you may have felt like an odd ball amidst the ones that are supposed to love you.

- At some point you may have felt like a mistake that they just had to keep.

- At some point you may have felt as if everyone and everything around you is against you.

- At some point you may have felt unworthy, and it made you question why God created you.

Why do you feel this way? Why is life so against you? Understand that you are a light so bright, and you are created for a purpose that will make the earth tremble. You are created different from your peers because you are the 'bible' that they read that convicts their sinful lifestyles, your words are the words that they envy and want to speak, and the spirit in you is what they seek.

Listen, before you were born, before you were formed in your mother's womb, God already created you. He did not create a mediocre type of human being in you. He created you to impact the world, your immediate environment; history will speak of your name and those who believe that your future is dim will testify about how great you have become and how bright your light shines.

You are a child of God; the world has no say in your future and cannot predict your destination in life because it is hidden in Christ. Therefore, allow the things that God will do in and through you to surprise them beyond measure as you develop your relationship with God. Let them speak; they will soon be quiet. Do not let mere humans, who cannot read the lines on your palm, or the lines on your face tell you that you are unworthy, do not allow empty souls seeking to bring others down, bring you down. You are a precious jewel, formed in the image of God, designed to be more precious than diamonds or gold. Understand that you were not created to be "liked;" you were created to *LEAD*, to *RULE*, and to *IMPACT*.

You were created for a purpose; you are more than a conqueror.

YOU ARE WORTHY!

Action Point – Let Us Pray:

- Oh Lord, forgive me for feeling unworthy. Help me to appreciate that You have created me to have more value than anything here on earth.
- Lord show Yourself in my life and help me remember every day of my life that I am worthy because You are worthy.

Abimbola Adekansola

10. The Reflection in the Mirror

So God created human beings in his own image.
In the image of God, He created them; male and female he created them.

Genesis 1:27 NLT

The sweet sound of the bird comes through the windows and gracefully reaches my ears as the sun begins to rise. The sound of the wind swiftly brushing the trees is comforting. I can lie here all day but there is work to be done. I open my eyes, get out of the bed, and walk to the restroom; morning has come. As I step out of the restroom, I see the reflection I have always dreaded.

As I look in the mirror I begin to hear those words *LOUD* and *CLEAR* - you are ugly, you are nothing, and will never amount to anything. You're a failure and a disgrace, no one will ever want you or love you; you are better off dead. As I stare at the mirror, I see the scars of pain. I see a broken-hearted failure with shattered hopes and a crushed future. The louder the words get, the more I shrink. My shirt is so tear-soaked. I have none left to cry, no more tears. My only thought is of *God*, so I begin to cry to Him: *"God help me! Please, God, help me. Father, Lord, help me! Help me! Help me!"* I close my eyes and suddenly I find myself before the mirror again, but this time the words that I hear are softer, comforting, and reassuring.

The whispers begin to make sense: You are *the radiance of my own glory. You express my very character.*[139] *The scars that you see are a reminder of how I brought you through the last time. I left them there so that you will know that if I did it before I can do it again.* Without those scars you wouldn't have a story. If I didn't place them there you wouldn't remember to call on me when you were unsure, hopeless, sad, or in need. You see pain in your scars but open your eyes and you will see power, strength, endurance, and patience. You see failure in your journey but I see perseverance, courage, and success. What you see makes you lose hope but look beyond and see a future full of glory, splendour, capability, talent, and skill.

Action Point - Reflection:

Listen, it is essential to *"be alert and of [a] sober mind, for the enemy prowls like a roaring lion looking for someone to devour. Resist him standing in faith..."*[140] He will use his tricky ways to try and fill your heart with lies which he knows you once believed, he will have the capacity to shift your focus from the mission that He has given you. You will not be able to focus on the dreams and the great plans that He has for your life. Resist the devil today! Tell him that he has no space in your life, your heart, and your mind.

Mercy Fakoya

---

[139] Hebrew 1:3
[140] 1 Peter 5:8-9

Spring Forth Devotional Checklist

Part 1 - SPRING

- ☐ God, My Strength
- ☐ Come Alive
- ☐ Now is the time
- ☐ The Overflow
- ☐ The Great Healer
- ☐ Choose Today
- ☐ Mold Me
- ☐ The Potter Process/Plan
- ☐ The Latter Rain
- ☐ Rejection
- ☐ Confidence in Christ
- ☐ No More Condemnation
- ☐ Choose Wisely
- ☐ My Help
- ☐ Beauty Beyond the Box
- ☐ Joy Over Jericho
- ☐ Christ-Like Character
- ☐ Change the Game
- ☐ Silence
- ☐ Wisdom from Above

Part 2 - FORWARD

- ☐ What's Love Got to Do With It?
- ☐ It's all about You Jesus
- ☐ Ceaseless Prayer
- ☐ Jesus, Where Are You?
- ☐ Hiding the word
- ☐ Heavenly Wealth
- ☐ Loving Others
- ☐ Are You a Thornbush?
- ☐ Who Do You Look Like?
- ☐ The Cup
- ☐ Procrastination Playground
- ☐ First Love
- ☐ The Power of Passion
- ☐ Follow-Follow
- ☐ Compromised Intimacy
- ☐ The Presence of God
- ☐ Praying with Purpose
- ☐ Trusting Love
- ☐ The Possibility of Holiness
- ☐ In His Image

Part 3 - EMERGE

- ☐ To Worship You I Live
- ☐ The Radiance of God
- ☐ Outliving The Flesh
- ☐ Righteousness a Gift!
- ☐ The Mind is A Battlefield
- ☐ The Power of Sharing
- ☐ The Mask
- ☐ New Season Shift
- ☐ Worthy
- ☐ The Reflection in the Mirror

Final Note:

We would love to connect with you and invite you to share your thoughts, quotes, nuggets and inspirations on your social media platforms as you read through this devotional handbook using the **hashtag:**

#Springforth

#SpringforthDevotional

Connecting with us will mean that you will be notified of any future resources that we release. We will also be starting some new initiatives and programmes with some of our friends (which we hope would include you); our virtual connection enables you to take advantage of and be a part of those future programmes and initiatives.

Our contact details:

Mercy Fakoya

- *MercyFakoya.com*
- *Twitter & Instagram: @itsgodsmercy*
- *Facebook & YouVersion: @MercyFakoya*
- *Ministry on Instagram & Twitter: @royalcitizens.org*
- *Business on Instagram: @mywwwcenter.com*

Debbie Akinkunle

- *DebbieAkinkunle.com*
- *Twitter: @TweetDebz*
- *Facebook, Instagram & YouVersion: @DebbieAkinkunle*
- *Ministry on Instagram: @WisdomTruthMinistries*
- *Business on Instagram & Twitter: @MinistersDesk*

Printed in Poland
by Amazon Fulfillment
Poland Sp. z o.o., Wrocław

52621558R00075